Plant-Based Slow Cooker Cookbook for Beginners

150 Slow Cooking Recipes for Everyday Cooking. Elevate Your Vegan Lifestyle with Quick, Nutrient-packed Meals

Table of contents

Benefits of a Plant-Based Diet

In recent years, the popularity of plant-based diets has surged as people become increasingly conscious of their health, the environment, and animal welfare. A plant-based diet involves consuming predominantly plant-derived foods while minimizing or eliminating animal products. This shift in dietary choices has been met with widespread enthusiasm, not just from vegans and vegetarians but also from individuals seeking a healthier and more sustainable lifestyle. The benefits of a plant-based diet extend far beyond personal well-being, encompassing environmental and ethical considerations as well.

One of the primary advantages of adopting a plant-based diet is its positive impact on heart health. Numerous studies have shown that plant-based diets can reduce the risk of cardiovascular diseases. The high fiber content, coupled with the absence of saturated fats found in many animal products, helps lower cholesterol levels and maintain healthy blood pressure. A diet rich in fruits, vegetables, whole grains, and nuts contributes to improved cardiovascular function, reducing the likelihood of heart-related issues.

Plant-based diets are often associated with effective weight management and weight loss. The emphasis on nutrient-dense, low-calorie foods means individuals can enjoy satisfying meals while consuming fewer overall calories. Additionally, plant-based diets are typically higher in fiber, promoting feelings of fullness and reducing the likelihood of overeating. This can be particularly beneficial for those looking to achieve or maintain a healthy weight.

Research consistently suggests that a plant-based diet is linked to a reduced risk of various chronic diseases, including type 2 diabetes, certain cancers, and hypertension. The abundance of antioxidants, vitamins, and minerals found in plant-based foods strengthens the immune system and supports overall health, creating a natural defense against chronic conditions.

A plant-based diet is inherently rich in dietary fiber, promoting optimal digestive health. Fiber aids in maintaining regular bowel movements, preventing constipation, and fostering a healthy gut microbiome. A balanced and diverse plant-based diet encourages the growth of beneficial bacteria in the digestive tract, contributing to improved digestion and nutrient absorption.

Beyond personal health benefits, choosing a plant-based diet can have a positive impact on the environment. Animal agriculture is a significant contributor to deforestation, water pollution, and greenhouse gas emissions. By opting for plant-based alternatives, individuals can reduce their ecological footprint, conserve water, and mitigate the environmental impact associated with industrial animal farming.

For many individuals, the decision to adopt a plant-based diet is rooted in ethical considerations regarding the treatment of animals. Choosing plant-based foods helps decrease the demand for animal products, leading to reduced reliance on factory farming practices. This aligns with a growing societal awareness of animal welfare issues and supports a more compassionate approach to food consumption.

The benefits of a plant-based diet extend far beyond the confines of personal health, encompassing environmental sustainability and ethical considerations. By embracing a diet rich in fruits, vegetables, whole grains, and legumes, individuals can enhance their well-being while contributing to a healthier planet. Whether motivated by health concerns, environmental consciousness, or ethical principles, the shift toward plant-based living represents a positive step toward a more sustainable and compassionate future.

Embracing a Plant-Based Lifestyle

In a contemporary world increasingly valuing health-conscious choices and sustainable living, the plant-based lifestyle has emerged as a powerful and transformative choice. Whether driven by health considerations, environmental consciousness, or ethical beliefs, adopting a plant-based diet can be a fulfilling and rewarding journey. To guide you through this lifestyle change, we present an extensive set of tips to help you embrace a plant-based diet with confidence and ease.

Educate Yourself on Nutrition. Commence your plant-based journey by delving deep into the understanding of the nutritional requirements of your body. Immerse yourself in the knowledge of essential nutrients found in plant-based foods and how to achieve a well-balanced diet. Familiarize yourself with sources of protein, iron, calcium, vitamin B12, and omega-3 fatty acids in the vast array of plant offerings.

Gradual Transition. A gradual transition can be more sustainable and comfortable, acting as a gentle introduction to the world of plant-based eating. Begin by incorporating one or two plant-based meals into your week, and progressively elevate the frequency as you become more accustomed to the lifestyle. This measured approach allows for a smoother adjustment, both for your evolving taste buds and your digestive system.

Diversify Your Plate. Embark on a culinary adventure by exploring the incredible variety of plant-based foods available. From the rainbow hues of vibrant fruits and vegetables to the heartiness of whole grains, legumes, nuts, and seeds, diversifying your plate ensures a broad spectrum of nutrients and keeps your meals exciting, enticing both your palate and your senses.

Optimize Plant-Based Protein Sources. Ensure you meet your protein requirements by strategically incorporating a diverse range of plant-based protein sources. From the humble beans and lentils to the versatile tofu, tempeh, quinoa, and edamame, enrich your meals with a mosaic of proteins. Combining different protein sources throughout the day helps ensure a complete amino acid profile, supporting your body's needs.

Prioritize Whole Foods. Elevate your commitment to health by placing a premium on whole, minimally processed foods. Let whole grains, fresh fruits, vegetables, and legumes take center stage, providing not only essential vitamins, minerals, and fiber but also contributing to a sense of satiety and sustained energy throughout the day.

Mindful Nutrient Intake. While a plant-based diet is inherently rich in nutrients, adopt a proactive stance by paying careful attention to specific vitamins and minerals that may require additional consideration. Consider incorporating supplements for nutrients like vitamin B12, vitamin D, and omega-3 fatty acids, which may be less abundant in plant-based diets.

Strategic Meal Planning. Navigate your culinary journey with foresight by strategically planning your meals. Craft a diverse menu that seamlessly integrates a mix of protein sources, a vibrant array of colorful vegetables, wholesome whole grains, and nourishing healthy fats. Preparing meals in advance not only saves time but also reduces the likelihood of opting for less healthy, convenience-driven choices.

Label Reading Awareness. Develop a keen eye for label scrutiny to identify any hidden animal products or undesirable additives. Cultivate familiarity with alternative names for animal-derived ingredients, empowering yourself to make informed and conscious choices while navigating the aisles of packaged foods. Your commitment to label reading ensures your dietary choices align with your plant-based principles.

Hydration is Key. Amplify your well-being by staying adequately hydrated through intentional consumption of water-rich fruits and vegetables, invigorating herbal teas, and refreshing infused water. Proper hydration is a cornerstone of digestive health, nutrient absorption, and overall vitality, ensuring you are poised to thrive in your plant-based lifestyle.

Connect with the Plant-Based Community. Elevate your journey by forging connections with a supportive community. Engage with like-minded individuals through vibrant social media groups, attend local meetups, or participate in online forums. Sharing experiences, triumphs, and tips with others on a similar journey not only fosters a sense of community but also enriches your plant-based experience, making the transition more enjoyable and sustainable.

Adopting a plant-based lifestyle transcends a mere dietary shift; it's a holistic approach to well-being that can positively impact your health, the environment, and animal welfare. By immersing yourself in education, embracing a gradual transition, and staying mindful of your nutritional needs, you can embark on this transformative journey with confidence and experience the manifold benefits of a plant-powered life.

Tips for Effective Slow Cooking

Going deeper into the idea of this book serving as a guide for slow cooker recipes, let's delve into additional insights to boost the success of your culinary journey. These tips are designed to streamline your cooking process and enhance the flavors and textures of your dishes. Whether you're an experienced slow cooker enthusiast or a beginner, integrating these suggestions can contribute to a more enjoyable and satisfying cooking experience.

When choosing a slow cooker, consider your specific needs. Opt for a larger size if you plan on batch cooking or preparing meals for the whole family. This is especially convenient for hearty stews or large cuts of meat. Conversely, if you're cooking for smaller portions or experimenting with new recipes, a smaller slow cooker is more suitable. Customizing the size to your intended use ensures optimal results and makes your slow cooking experience more efficient and enjoyable.

Efficiency is crucial in slow cooking, and preparing ingredients the night before can significantly streamline your mornings. Take the time in the evening to chop vegetables, marinate meats, or measure out spices. This foresight allows you to assemble your meal quickly in the morning, minimizing the rush and making the start of your slow cooking process smooth and stress-free. This simple yet effective tip not only saves time but also ensures that you can savor a delicious, well-prepared meal with minimal morning hassle.

Achieving even cooking in your slow cooker is an art, and strategic layering plays a crucial role. Place meats at the bottom of the slow cooker and delicate vegetables on top to ensure optimal results. This method allows the meat to absorb flavors from the ingredients below while preventing the vegetables from becoming overly mushy during the extended cooking process. By mastering the art of ingredient layering, you enhance the overall taste and texture of your slow-cooked dishes.

In the realm of slow cooking, managing liquid levels is pivotal. Unlike traditional cooking methods, slow cookers require less liquid. When adapting a recipe from stovetop or oven cooking to the slow cooker, it's essential to reduce the amount of liquid used. This adjustment ensures that your slow-cooked dishes achieve the desired consistency and intensity of flavors. By being mindful of liquid levels, you not only embrace the unique dynamics of slow cooking but also guarantee that your creations are perfectly balanced and rich in taste, making the most out of every ingredient.

Maintaining a closed lid is a cardinal rule in slow cooking. Every time you lift the lid, valuable heat escapes, and this can substantially extend the cooking time. Resist the temptation to peek unnecessarily. Only open the lid when essential tasks like stirring or adding ingredients midway are required. This discipline preserves the consistent heat and ensures that your slow cooker functions optimally, resulting in perfectly cooked and flavorful dishes. By embracing this patience-driven approach, you contribute to the success of your slow-cooked creations, achieving the desired tenderness and melding of flavors without unnecessary disruptions.

Precision in temperature is a key factor in successful slow cooking. Adhere to the temperature guidelines specified in your recipe. Opting for the low setting and allowing for a more extended cooking period often leads to tender and more flavorful results. This gentle, prolonged cooking process allows flavors to meld, and tougher cuts of meat to become succulent. By respecting the suggested temperature settings, you harness the full potential of your slow cooker, ensuring that each dish reaches its peak of tenderness and taste.

When incorporating dairy into your slow-cooked dishes, timing is crucial to avoid unwanted curdling. Milk or cream should be stirred in during the last 15-30 minutes of the cooking process. Adding dairy too early can lead to curdling due to the prolonged exposure to heat. By introducing dairy towards the end, you preserve its creamy texture and enhance the overall richness of your dish. This careful timing ensures that your slow-cooked creations maintain a smooth and luscious consistency, delivering a delightful and well-balanced culinary experience.

Elevate the freshness and aroma of your slow-cooked dishes by incorporating fresh herbs towards the end of the cooking time. Their delicate flavors are best preserved when added closer to completion. On the other hand, dried herbs can be introduced earlier in the process, allowing their robust notes to infuse gradually. This thoughtful approach ensures that the essence of fresh herbs enhances your dish, providing a burst of flavor right before serving. By mastering the timing of herb additions, you infuse your slow-cooked meals with a harmonious blend of fragrances that captivate the palate.

Achieving the perfect consistency is key in slow cooking. If your dish is too watery, employ strategic methods to enhance thickness. Firstly, uncover the slow cooker for the last 30 minutes of cooking to allow some moisture to evaporate and the sauce to naturally thicken. Alternatively, for more immediate results, consider creating a slurry by mixing cornstarch with water. Stir this slurry into your dish, and the sauce will thicken as it continues to simmer. This versatile technique empowers you to fine-tune the texture of your slow-cooked creations, ensuring a satisfying and well-balanced culinary experience.

Simplify your post-cooking routine by adopting a proactive approach to cleanup. Consider using slow cooker liners or spraying the interior with non-stick cooking spray before adding ingredients. Slow cooker liners provide a convenient barrier that makes cleanup a breeze, while a light coating of non-stick spray minimizes the chances of ingredients sticking to the surface. Embracing these easy cleanup practices ensures that the joy of slow cooking extends beyond the kitchen, allowing you to savor your delicious creations without the hassle of extensive scrubbing afterward.

By adhering to the advice provided above, you can optimize your cooking experience with a slow cooker. From selecting the right size to strategic ingredient preparation and managing liquid levels, these tips cover various aspects to ensure that your slow-cooked dishes are not only delicious but also prepared with efficiency and ease. Incorporating these practices will enhance your overall enjoyment of slow cooker cooking, making it a rewarding and convenient culinary experience.

Foundational
Broths &
Bases

Golden Turmeric Vegetable Broth

INGREDIENTS

- 6 cups of water
- 2 large carrots, roughly chopped
- 2 celery stalks, roughly chopped
- 1 medium onion, quartered
- 3 garlic cloves, smashed
- 2-inch piece of fresh ginger, sliced
- 2-inch piece of fresh turmeric, sliced (or 2 tsp of turmeric powder if fresh is unavailable)
- 1 tsp black peppercorns
- 1 bay leaf

  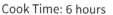

Prep Time: 15 min   Cook Time: 6 hours   Serves: 4

DIRECTIONS

Place all the ingredients, except salt and herbs, into the slow cooker. Fill the slow cooker with water, ensuring the vegetables are fully submerged. Cover and cook on low for 6 hours. About 30 minutes before turning off the cooker, add in the fresh herbs. Once done, strain out the solids and season the broth with salt to taste. Let it cool and then store in the refrigerator or use immediately.

NUTRITIONAL INFORMATION

Per serving: 35 calories, 1g protein, 8g carbohydrates, 0.5g fat, 2g fiber, 0mg cholesterol, 320mg sodium, 210mg potassium.

Savory Mushroom Stock

INGREDIENTS

- 6 cups of water
- 1 pound of mixed fresh mushrooms (like cremini, shiitake, and button), roughly chopped
- 1 large onion, quartered
- 3 garlic cloves, smashed
- 2 celery stalks, roughly chopped
- 1 large carrot, roughly chopped
- 1 bay leaf
- 10 black peppercorns
- 2 sprigs of fresh thyme

Prep Time: 20 min   Cook Time: 6 hours   Serves: 4

DIRECTIONS

Place all the ingredients, except salt and parsley, into the slow cooker. Fill the slow cooker with water, ensuring the ingredients are fully submerged. Cover and cook on low for 6 hours. About 30 minutes before finishing, add in the fresh parsley. Once done, strain out the solids and season the stock with salt to taste. Let it cool, then store in the refrigerator or use immediately.

NUTRITIONAL INFORMATION

Per serving: 45 calories, 3g protein, 10g carbohydrates, 0.3g fat, 3g fiber, 0mg cholesterol, 330mg sodium, 290mg potassium.

Herbal Elixir Broth

INGREDIENTS

- 6 cups of water
- 1 bunch of fresh parsley, roughly chopped
- 1 bunch of fresh cilantro, roughly chopped
- 3 sprigs of fresh rosemary
- 3 sprigs of fresh thyme
- 2 bay leaves
- 5-7 fresh basil leaves
- 2-inch piece of ginger, thinly sliced
- 1 lemon, thinly sliced (with rind)
- 10 black peppercorns

Prep Time: 10 min   Cook Time: 5 hours   Serves: 4

DIRECTIONS

Place all the ingredients, except salt, into the slow cooker. Fill the slow cooker with water, ensuring the herbs and spices are fully submerged. Cover and cook on low for 5 hours. Once done, strain out the solids and season the broth with salt to taste. Let it cool, then store in the refrigerator or use immediately. Before serving, add a splash of apple cider vinegar for an added zesty touch.

NUTRITIONAL INFORMATION

Per serving: 15 calories, 0.5g protein, 4g carbohydrates, 0.1g fat, 1g fiber, 0mg cholesterol, 310mg sodium, 80mg potassium.

Smoky Tomato Base

INGREDIENTS

- 6 cups of water
- 2 pounds of ripe tomatoes, roughly chopped
- 1 medium onion, roughly chopped
- 4 garlic cloves, smashed
- 2 red bell peppers, deseeded and roughly chopped
- 2 tsp smoked paprika
- 1 tsp dried oregano
- 1/2 tsp chipotle chili powder (adjust to taste)
- 1 tsp black peppercorns
- 1 tbsp apple cider vinegar

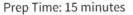

Prep Time: 15 minutes   Cook Time: 4 hours   Serves: 4

DIRECTIONS

In the slow cooker, combine tomatoes, onion, garlic, red bell peppers, smoked paprika, oregano, chipotle chili powder, peppercorns, and olive oil. Pour in the water and ensure all ingredients are submerged. Cover and cook on low for 4 hours. Once cooked, use an immersion blender or transfer to a stand blender to puree until smooth. Return to the slow cooker and stir in apple cider vinegar. Season with salt to taste. Let it cool, then store in the refrigerator or use as a base for other dishes.

NUTRITIONAL INFORMATION

Per serving: 90 calories, 2g protein, 14g carbohydrates, 3.5g fat, 3g fiber, 0mg cholesterol, 330mg sodium, 500mg potassium.

Sweet Potato & Ginger Infusion

INGREDIENTS

- 6 cups of water
- 2 medium sweet potatoes, peeled and roughly chopped
- 3-inch piece of ginger, thinly sliced
- 1 cinnamon stick
- 4 cardamom pods, slightly crushed
- 1/4 tsp ground nutmeg
- 1 star anise
- 1 tbsp maple syrup (optional, adjust to taste)
- Salt, to taste (start with a pinch and adjust at the end if needed)

 Prep Time: 15 minutes

 Cook Time: 5 hours

 Serves: 4

DIRECTIONS

Combine sweet potatoes, ginger slices, cinnamon stick, cardamom pods, nutmeg, star anise, and maple syrup (if using) in the slow cooker. Pour in the water, ensuring all ingredients are submerged. Cover and cook on low for 5 hours. Once done, strain out the solids. Season the infusion with a pinch of salt to taste and adjust sweetness if needed. Serve warm, and enjoy the comforting blend of sweet potato and aromatic spices.

NUTRITIONAL INFORMATION

Per serving: 110 calories, 2g protein, 26g carbohydrates, 0.2g fat, 3g fiber, 0mg cholesterol, 50mg sodium, 400mg potassium.

White Bean and Garlic Broth

INGREDIENTS

- 6 cups of water
- 1 cup dried white beans (like Cannellini or Great Northern), soaked overnight and drained
- 1 whole head of garlic, cloves separated and peeled
- 1 bay leaf
- 1 sprig of fresh rosemary
- 1 sprig of fresh thyme
- 10 black peppercorns
- 2 tbsp olive oil
- Salt, to taste (start with 1/2 tsp and adjust at the end if needed)

 Prep Time: 10 min

 Cook Time: 8 hours

 Serves: 4

DIRECTIONS

Place the soaked white beans, garlic cloves, bay leaf, rosemary, thyme, peppercorns, and olive oil into the slow cooker. Add the water, ensuring all ingredients are submerged. Cover and cook on low for 8 hours. Once cooked, strain out the solids. Season the broth with salt to taste. For a thicker consistency, you can blend a portion of the beans and garlic back into the broth. Serve warm, garnishing with a sprig of fresh herbs or a drizzle of olive oil if desired.

NUTRITIONAL INFORMATION

Per serving: 150 calories, 7g protein, 23g carbohydrates, 3g fat, 6g fiber, 0mg cholesterol, 320mg sodium, 600mg potassium.

Rosemary & Thyme Veggie Stock

INGREDIENTS

- 6 cups of water
- 2 carrots, roughly chopped
- 2 celery stalks, roughly chopped
- 1 onion, peeled and quartered
- 4 garlic cloves, smashed
- 2 sprigs fresh rosemary
- 3 sprigs fresh thyme
- 1 bay leaf
- 10 black peppercorns
- 1 small bunch parsley, roughly chopped
- 1 tbsp olive oil
- Salt, to taste (start with 1/2 tsp and adjust at the end if needed)

 Prep Time: 15 min

 Cook Time: 6 hours

 Serves: 4

DIRECTIONS

Place carrots, celery, onion, garlic, rosemary, thyme, bay leaf, peppercorns, parsley, and olive oil in the slow cooker. Pour in the water, ensuring all ingredients are covered. Cover and cook on low for 6 hours. After cooking, strain the stock through a fine-mesh sieve to remove solids. Season with salt to taste. Allow the stock to cool and then store in the refrigerator, or use immediately as a base for soups and stews.

NUTRITIONAL INFORMATION

Per serving: 40 calories, 1g protein, 7g carbohydrates, 1.5g fat, 2g fiber, 0mg cholesterol, 310mg sodium, 200mg potassium.

Roasted Red Pepper Liquid Gold

INGREDIENTS

- 6 cups of water
- 4 large red bell peppers, seeded and roughly chopped
- 1 medium onion, roughly chopped
- 5 garlic cloves, smashed
- 2 tsp smoked paprika
- 1 tsp dried basil
- 1/2 tsp red pepper flakes (adjust to taste)
- 1 bay leaf
- 10 black peppercorns
- 1 tbsp olive oil
- 1 tbsp apple cider vinegar or lemon juice

 Prep Time: 20 min

 Cook Time: 6 hours

 Serves: 4

DIRECTIONS

Combine red bell peppers, onion, garlic, smoked paprika, basil, red pepper flakes, bay leaf, peppercorns, and olive oil in the slow cooker. Pour in the water, making sure all ingredients are submerged. Cover and cook on low for 6 hours.

After cooking, use an immersion blender or transfer to a stand blender to puree until smooth. Stir in apple cider vinegar or lemon juice and season with salt to taste. Strain through a fine-mesh sieve if a clearer consistency is desired, and then store in the refrigerator or use immediately as a flavorful base for soups, sauces, or stews.

NUTRITIONAL INFORMATION

Per serving: 70 calories, 2g protein, 11g carbohydrates, 2.5g fat, 3g fiber, 0mg cholesterol, 330mg sodium, 320mg potassium.

Caramelized Onion Broth

INGREDIENTS

- 6 cups of water
- 5 large onions, thinly sliced
- 4 garlic cloves, smashed
- 1 tbsp olive oil
- 2 bay leaves
- 1 tsp dried thyme
- 10 black peppercorns
- Salt, to taste (start with 1/2 tsp and adjust at the end if needed)
- 1 tbsp balsamic vinegar or red wine vinegar

Prep Time: 10 min

Cook Time: 10 hours

Serves: 4

DIRECTIONS

In a large skillet over medium heat, add olive oil and thinly sliced onions. Cook until onions are deeply caramelized, approximately 20-25 minutes. Add garlic in the last 5 minutes to lightly brown. Transfer the caramelized onions and garlic to the slow cooker. Add bay leaves, thyme, peppercorns, and water. Cover and cook on low for 9 hours. After cooking, stir in balsamic or red wine vinegar and season with salt to taste. Strain the broth to remove solids before serving or using in recipes.

NUTRITIONAL INFORMATION

Per serving: 80 calories, 2g protein, 17g carbohydrates, 2g fat, 3g fiber, 0mg cholesterol, 310mg sodium, 260mg potassium.

Zesty Lemon and Herb Broth

INGREDIENTS

- 6 cups of water
- Zest and juice of 2 large lemons
- 1 cup fresh parsley, roughly chopped
- 1 cup fresh cilantro, roughly chopped
- 1 sprig of fresh rosemary
- 2 sprigs of fresh thyme
- 4 garlic cloves, smashed
- 1 tbsp olive oil
- 10 black peppercorns
- Salt, to taste (start with 1/2 tsp and adjust at the end if needed)

Prep Time: 15 min

Cook Time: 8 hours

Serves: 4 servings

DIRECTIONS

In the slow cooker, combine lemon zest, lemon juice, parsley, cilantro, rosemary, thyme, garlic, olive oil, and black peppercorns. Pour in the water, ensuring all ingredients are submerged. Cover and cook on low for 8 hours. After cooking, season with salt to taste. Strain the broth to remove solids before serving or using in recipes.

NUTRITIONAL INFORMATION

Per serving: 60 calories, 1g protein, 9g carbohydrates, 2.5g fat, 2g fiber, 0mg cholesterol, 290mg sodium, 180mg potassium.

Spicy Asian Broth Foundation

INGREDIENTS

- 6 cups of water
- 1-inch ginger root, sliced
- 4 garlic cloves, smashed
- 2 green onions, chopped (white and green parts separated)
- 2 dried red chili peppers (adjust to desired heat level)
- 1 tbsp soy sauce or tamari (for gluten-free)
- 1 tbsp rice vinegar
- 1 tsp toasted sesame oil
- 1 small piece kombu (seaweed, about 4 inches long)
- 10 black peppercorns
- Salt, to taste (start with 1/2 tsp and adjust at the end if needed)

Prep Time: 15 min

Cook Time: 8 hours

Serves: 4

DIRECTIONS

In the slow cooker, combine ginger, garlic, white parts of green onions, dried red chili peppers, soy sauce, rice vinegar, sesame oil, kombu, and black peppercorns. Pour in the water, ensuring all ingredients are submerged. Cover and cook on low for 8 hours. After cooking, season with salt to taste. Strain the broth to remove solids and garnish with the green parts of the green onions before serving or using in recipes.

NUTRITIONAL INFORMATION

Per serving: 40 calories, 1g protein, 6g carbohydrates, 1.5g fat, 1g fiber, 0mg cholesterol, 450mg sodium, 110mg potassium.

Lentil & Bay Leaf Stock

INGREDIENTS

- 6 cups of water
- 1 cup green lentils, rinsed and drained
- 2 bay leaves
- 1 onion, roughly chopped
- 2 carrots, chopped
- 3 celery stalks, chopped
- 4 garlic cloves, smashed
- 1 tsp black peppercorns
- 1 tbsp olive oil
- Salt, to taste (start with 1/2 tsp and adjust at the end if needed)

Prep Time: 10 min

Cook Time: 6 hours

Serves: 4

DIRECTIONS

In the slow cooker, combine lentils, bay leaves, onion, carrots, celery, garlic, peppercorns, and olive oil. Pour in the water, ensuring all ingredients are submerged. Cover and cook on low for 6 hours. After cooking, season with salt to taste. Strain the stock to remove solids before using in recipes.

NUTRITIONAL INFORMATION

Per serving: 130 calories, 8g protein, 23g carbohydrates, 1.5g fat, 9g fiber, 0mg cholesterol, 320mg sodium, 450mg potassium.

Toasted Corn & Cilantro Broth

INGREDIENTS

- 6 cups of water
- 2 cups fresh corn kernels (from about 2 large ears of corn)
- 1 cup fresh cilantro, roughly chopped
- 1 onion, roughly chopped
- 2 garlic cloves, minced
- 1 green chili pepper, seeded and chopped (optional for added heat)
- 1 tbsp olive oil
- Salt and pepper, to taste

Prep Time: 15 min

Cook Time: 6 hours

Serves: 4

DIRECTIONS

In a skillet over medium heat, add the corn kernels. Toast them, stirring frequently, until they are golden brown (about 5-7 minutes). Transfer the toasted corn to the slow cooker and add cilantro, onion, garlic, chili pepper (if using), and olive oil. Pour in the water, ensuring all ingredients are submerged.

Cover and cook on low for 6 hours. After cooking, season with salt and pepper to taste. Strain the broth to remove solids before using or serving.

NUTRITIONAL INFORMATION

Per serving: 115 calories, 3g protein, 21g carbohydrates, 3.5g fat, 2g fiber, 0mg cholesterol, 180mg sodium, 320mg potassium.

Hearty Kale & Seaweed Broth

INGREDIENTS

- 6 cups of water
- 2 cups fresh kale, washed and roughly chopped
- 1 cup dried seaweed (like kombu or wakame), rehydrated in warm water and chopped
- 1 onion, sliced
- 3 garlic cloves, minced
- 2 tbsp tamari or soy sauce
- 1 tbsp miso paste (optional)
- 1 tbsp olive oil
- Salt and pepper, to taste

Prep Time: 10 min

Cook Time: 6 hours

Serves: 4

DIRECTIONS

In a skillet over medium heat, sauté the onions in olive oil until translucent. Add garlic and continue sautéing for another minute. Transfer the onions and garlic to the slow cooker. Add the kale, rehydrated seaweed, tamari (or soy sauce), and miso paste. Pour in the water, ensuring all ingredients are submerged. Cover and cook on low for 6 hours. After cooking, season with salt and pepper to taste. Strain the broth to remove solids before using or serving.

NUTRITIONAL INFORMATION

Per serving: 80 calories, 4g protein, 12g carbohydrates, 2g fat, 3g fiber, 0mg cholesterol, 700mg sodium, 450mg potassium.

Beetroot & Star Anise Infusion

INGREDIENTS

- 4 medium beetroots, peeled and sliced
- 6 cups of water
- 3-4 star anise
- 1 small red onion, thinly sliced
- 2 garlic cloves, minced
- 1 tablespoon apple cider vinegar
- Salt and pepper, to taste
- 1 tablespoon olive oil

Prep Time: 15 min

Cook Time: 5 hours

Serves: 4

DIRECTIONS

In a skillet over medium heat, sauté the onions and garlic in olive oil until translucent. Transfer the onions and garlic to the slow cooker. Add beetroot slices, star anise, and apple cider vinegar. Pour in the water, ensuring all ingredients are submerged. Cover and cook on low for 5 hours. Once cooked, season with salt and pepper to taste. Strain the infusion to remove solids before serving.

NUTRITIONAL INFORMATION

Per serving: 70 calories, 2g protein, 15g carbohydrates, 2g fat, 3g fiber, 0mg cholesterol, 120mg sodium, 400mg potassium.

Hearty Soups
& Stews

Tuscan White Bean & Kale Soup

INGREDIENTS

- 2 cups white beans (cannellini beans), soaked overnight and drained
- 6 cups vegetable broth
- 1 large onion, diced
- 3 cloves garlic, minced
- 1 medium carrot, sliced
- 1 celery stalk, sliced
- 4 cups kale, stemmed and chopped
- 1 can (14 oz.) diced tomatoes, drained
- 2 teaspoons olive oil
- 1 teaspoon dried thyme
- 1 bay leaf

Prep Time: 20 min

Cook Time: 6 hours

Serves: 4

DIRECTIONS

In a skillet over medium heat, sauté the onions, garlic, carrots, and celery in olive oil until softened, about 5 minutes. Transfer the sautéed vegetables to the slow cooker. Add beans, vegetable broth, diced tomatoes, thyme, bay leaf, and kale. Cover and cook on low for 6 hours, or until beans are tender. Season with salt, pepper, and fresh lemon juice. Stir well. Serve hot, garnished with fresh basil or parsley.

NUTRITIONAL INFORMATION

Per serving: 220 calories, 13g protein, 38g carbohydrates, 3g fat, 8g fiber, 0mg cholesterol, 400mg sodium, 650mg potassium.

Moroccan Lentil & Chickpea Stew

INGREDIENTS

- 1 cup dried lentils, rinsed and drained
- 1 can (14 oz.) chickpeas, drained and rinsed
- 1 large onion, diced
- 3 cloves garlic, minced
- 2 large carrots, diced
- 2 celery stalks, diced
- 1 red bell pepper, chopped
- 1 can (14 oz.) diced tomatoes
- 4 cups vegetable broth
- 2 teaspoons ground cumin
- 1 teaspoon ground turmeric, cinnamon
- 1/2 teaspoon ground ginger
- 1/4 teaspoon cayenne pepper (optional, for heat)

Prep Time: 15 minutes

Cook Time: 7 hours

Serves: 4

DIRECTIONS

In the slow cooker, combine lentils, chickpeas, onions, garlic, carrots, celery, bell pepper, and diced tomatoes. Add in vegetable broth, cumin, turmeric, cinnamon, ginger, cayenne pepper, salt, and pepper. Stir to mix all ingredients.

Cover and cook on low for 7 hours or until lentils are tender. Before serving, adjust seasoning if needed and garnish with freshly chopped cilantro or parsley.

NUTRITIONAL INFORMATION

Per serving: 280 calories, 16g protein, 48g carbohydrates, 2g fat, 15g fiber, 0mg cholesterol, 600mg sodium, 800mg potassium.

Hearty Vegetable & Barley Soup

INGREDIENTS

- 1/2 cup pearled barley, rinsed and drained
- 1 cup carrots, diced
- 1 cup celery, diced
- 1 large onion, diced
- 2 cloves garlic, minced
- 1 cup green beans, chopped
- 1 red bell pepper, diced
- 1 can (14 oz.) diced tomatoes, undrained
- 5 cups vegetable broth
- 1 teaspoon dried oregano
- 1/2 teaspoon dried thyme
- 2 bay leaves
- 1 cup kale or spinach, chopped

Prep Time: 15 min

Cook Time: 6 hours

Serves: 4

DIRECTIONS

In the slow cooker, combine barley, carrots, celery, onion, garlic, green beans, bell pepper, and diced tomatoes. Add vegetable broth, oregano, thyme, salt, pepper, and bay leaves. Stir to combine. Cover and cook on low for 5.5 hours. Add kale or spinach and cook for another 30 minutes or until barley and vegetables are tender. Before serving, discard bay leaves, adjust seasoning if needed, and garnish with freshly chopped parsley.

NUTRITIONAL INFORMATION

Per serving: 220 calories, 7g protein, 45g carbohydrates, 1g fat, 10g fiber, 0mg cholesterol, 720mg sodium, 600mg potassium.

Creamy Butternut Squash Bisque

INGREDIENTS

- 1 medium butternut squash, peeled, seeded, and chopped
- 1 medium onion, diced
- 2 cloves garlic, minced
- 4 cups vegetable broth
- 1 can (14 oz.) coconut milk
- 1/2 teaspoon dried sage
- 1/4 teaspoon nutmeg
- 1/2 teaspoon sea salt (adjust to taste)
- 1/4 teaspoon black pepper (adjust to taste)
- Optional toppings: pumpkin seeds, chopped fresh parsley, or a drizzle of coconut milk

Prep Time: 15 min

Cook Time: 6 hours

Serves: 4

DIRECTIONS

Place butternut squash, onion, garlic, and vegetable broth into the slow cooker. Cover and cook on low for 5-6 hours or until the squash is tender. Using an immersion blender, puree the soup until smooth. Alternatively, transfer the mixture to a blender and blend until smooth, then return it to the slow cooker. Stir in coconut milk, sage, nutmeg, salt, and pepper. Heat on low for another 15 minutes to meld flavors. Serve hot and garnish with optional toppings if desired.

NUTRITIONAL INFORMATION

Per serving: 220 calories, 4g protein, 32g carbohydrates, 9g fat, 5g fiber, 0mg cholesterol, 500mg sodium, 600mg potassium.

Spicy Black Bean & Quinoa Chili

INGREDIENTS

- 1 cup dry black beans, rinsed and soaked overnight
- 1/2 cup uncooked quinoa, rinsed and drained
- 1 large onion, diced
- 2 cloves garlic, minced
- 1 red bell pepper, diced
- 2 jalapeños, seeds removed and finely diced
- 1 can (14 oz.) diced tomatoes, with their juice
- 4 cups vegetable broth
- 2 teaspoons ground cumin
- 1 teaspoon smoked paprika
- 1/2 teaspoon cayenne pepper

Prep Time: 20 min

Cook Time: 6 hours

Serves: 4

DIRECTIONS

In the slow cooker, combine black beans, quinoa, onion, garlic, bell pepper, jalapeños, diced tomatoes, and vegetable broth. Stir in cumin, smoked paprika, cayenne pepper, salt, and black pepper. Cover and cook on low for 5-6 hours or until beans are tender and quinoa is cooked. Before serving, taste and adjust seasoning if necessary. Serve hot, garnished with fresh cilantro if desired.

NUTRITIONAL INFORMATION

Per serving: 310 calories, 15g protein, 58g carbohydrates, 3g fat, 13g fiber, 0mg cholesterol, 420mg sodium, 700mg potassium.

Wild Rice & Mushroom Stew

INGREDIENTS

- 1 cup uncooked wild rice, rinsed and drained
- 1 pound mixed mushrooms (like cremini, shiitake, and oyster), sliced
- 1 large onion, diced
- 3 cloves garlic, minced
- 1 carrot, diced
- 2 celery stalks, diced
- 4 cups vegetable broth
- 2 bay leaves
- 1 teaspoon dried thyme
- 1/2 cup unsweetened almond milk
- 2 tablespoons nutritional yeast

Prep Time: 15 min

Cook Time: 7 hours

Serves: 4

DIRECTIONS

In the slow cooker, combine wild rice, mushrooms, onion, garlic, carrot, and celery. Pour in the vegetable broth and add bay leaves, thyme, salt, and black pepper. Cover and cook on low for 6-7 hours, or until the rice is tender. In the last 30 minutes of cooking, stir in almond milk and nutritional yeast (if using) to add creaminess. Serve hot, garnished with fresh parsley.

NUTRITIONAL INFORMATION

Per serving: 260 calories, 10g protein, 48g carbohydrates, 3g fat, 6g fiber, 0mg cholesterol, 600mg sodium, 450mg potassium.

Thai Coconut & Tofu Curry Soup

INGREDIENTS

- 1 can (14 oz) full-fat coconut milk
- 4 cups vegetable broth
- 200g firm tofu, cubed
- 2 tablespoons red curry paste
- 1 medium onion, thinly sliced
- 2 cloves garlic, minced
- 1 tablespoon freshly grated ginger
- 1 red bell pepper, sliced
- 1 cup sliced bamboo shoots
- 1 cup chopped bok choy or baby spinach
- 1 tablespoon soy sauce or tamari, coconut sugar or brown sugar

Prep Time: 20 min

Cook Time: 4 hours

Serves: 4

DIRECTIONS

In the slow cooker, whisk together the coconut milk, vegetable broth, and red curry paste until smooth. Add in tofu cubes, onion, garlic, ginger, red bell pepper, bamboo shoots, and chili pepper if using. Cover and cook on low for 3-4 hours. In the last 30 minutes of cooking, stir in bok choy (or spinach), soy sauce, lime juice, and sugar. Serve hot, garnished with fresh cilantro and green onions.

NUTRITIONAL INFORMATION

Per serving: 320 calories, 12g protein, 25g carbohydrates, 21g fat, 3g fiber, 0mg cholesterol, 680mg sodium, 620mg potassium.

Potato & Spinach Chowder

INGREDIENTS

- 4 large potatoes, peeled and diced
- 1 medium onion, chopped
- 2 cloves garlic, minced
- 4 cups vegetable broth
- 1 cup unsweetened almond milk or any plant-based milk
- 2 cups fresh spinach, roughly chopped
- 1 teaspoon dried thyme
- 1/2 teaspoon dried rosemary
- 1 tablespoon olive oil or coconut oil
- Fresh chives, for garnish

Prep Time: 15 min

Cook Time: 6 hours

Serves: 4

DIRECTIONS

In the slow cooker, combine potatoes, onion, garlic, thyme, rosemary, salt, pepper, and vegetable broth. Cover and cook on low for 5-6 hours, or until the potatoes are tender. About 30 minutes before serving, add in the almond milk and spinach, stirring to combine. Before serving, use an immersion blender to partially blend the chowder, leaving some potato chunks for texture. Alternatively, you can transfer half the soup to a blender, blend until smooth, and then return to the slow cooker. Serve hot, garnished with fresh chives.

NUTRITIONAL INFORMATION

Per serving: 230 calories, 6g protein, 50g carbohydrates, 3g fat, 7g fiber, 0mg cholesterol, 800mg sodium, 1100mg potassium.

Three-Bean Vegetable Medley

INGREDIENTS

- 1 cup kidney beans, soaked overnight and drained
- 1 cup black beans, soaked overnight and drained
- 1 cup white beans (like cannellini or navy), soaked overnight and drained
- 4 cups vegetable broth
- 1 large carrot, diced
- 1 medium onion, chopped
- 2 cloves garlic, minced
- 2 celery stalks, diced
- 1 bell pepper, diced
- 1 zucchini, diced
- 1 cup diced tomatoes
- 2 teaspoons dried oregano
- 1 teaspoon dried basil

Prep Time: 20 min   Cook Time: 6 hours   Serves: 6

DIRECTIONS

In the slow cooker, combine kidney beans, black beans, white beans, carrot, onion, garlic, celery, bell pepper, zucchini, and tomatoes. Add in the vegetable broth, oregano, basil, salt, and pepper. Drizzle with olive oil and give a good stir to combine all the ingredients. Cover and cook on low for 6 hours or until the beans are tender and flavors melded. Adjust seasoning if necessary, and serve warm with crusty bread or a salad on the side.

NUTRITIONAL INFORMATION

Per serving: 280 calories, 15g protein, 45g carbohydrates, 4g fat, 12g fiber, 0mg cholesterol, 450mg sodium, 850mg potassium.

Roasted Eggplant & Bell Pepper Stew

INGREDIENTS

- 2 large eggplants, diced into 1-inch cubes
- 3 bell peppers (red, yellow, and green), seeded and chopped
- 1 medium onion, chopped
- 3 cloves garlic, minced
- 1 can (14 oz) diced tomatoes, with juices
- 3 cups vegetable broth
- 2 teaspoons dried oregano
- 1 teaspoon dried basil
- 1/2 teaspoon smoked paprika

Prep Time: 25 min   Cook Time: 4 hours   Serves: 4

DIRECTIONS

Preheat oven to 425°F (220°C). Place the diced eggplant and chopped bell peppers on a baking sheet. Drizzle with olive oil and season with salt and pepper. Roast for 15-20 minutes, or until slightly charred. Transfer the roasted eggplant and peppers to the slow cooker. Add onion, garlic, diced tomatoes, vegetable broth, oregano, dried basil, and smoked paprika. Cover and cook on low for 4 hours. Season with salt and pepper to taste. Garnish with fresh basil or parsley if desired. Serve warm with crusty bread or a side salad.

NUTRITIONAL INFORMATION

Per serving: 180 calories, 4g protein, 35g carbohydrates, 5g fat, 9g fiber, 0mg cholesterol, 600mg sodium, 650mg potassium.

Red Lentil & Spinach Dahl

INGREDIENTS

- 1 cup red lentils, rinsed and drained
- 1 large onion, finely chopped
- 3 cloves garlic, minced
- 1 tablespoon ginger, grated
- 2 cups spinach, washed and roughly chopped
- 1 can (14 oz) diced tomatoes
- 3 cups vegetable broth
- 2 teaspoons ground turmeric
- 1 teaspoon ground cumin, ground coriander
- 1/2 teaspoon chili powder
- 2 tablespoons coconut oil

Prep Time: 15 min   Cook Time: 6 hours   Serves: 4

DIRECTIONS

In a skillet, heat the coconut oil and sauté the onions until translucent. Add garlic and ginger, and cook for another 2 minutes. Transfer the onion mixture to the slow cooker. Add red lentils, diced tomatoes, vegetable broth, turmeric, cumin, coriander, and chili powder. Cover and cook on low for 5 hours. Stir in the chopped spinach and cook for another hour or until lentils are soft and creamy. Garnish with fresh cilantro and serve with rice or naan.

NUTRITIONAL INFORMATION

Per serving: 250 calories, 15g protein, 38g carbohydrates, 5g fat, 15g fiber, 0mg cholesterol, 600mg sodium, 700mg potassium.

Sweet Corn & Zucchini Soup

INGREDIENTS

- 3 cups fresh sweet corn kernels (from about 4 cobs)
- 2 medium zucchinis, diced
- 1 medium onion, finely chopped
- 2 cloves garlic, minced
- 1 tablespoon olive oil
- 4 cups vegetable broth
- 1/2 cup coconut milk
- Salt and pepper to taste
- Fresh herbs (like basil or parsley) for garnish, chopped (optional)

Prep Time: 20 min   Cook Time: 4 hours   Serves: 4

DIRECTIONS

In a skillet, heat the olive oil and sauté the onions until translucent. Add garlic and cook for another 1-2 minutes. Transfer the onion and garlic mixture to the slow cooker. Add sweet corn, zucchinis, and vegetable broth. Cover and cook on low for 3.5 hours. Add coconut milk, season with salt and pepper, and continue cooking for another 30 minutes. Garnish with fresh herbs before serving, if desired.

NUTRITIONAL INFORMATION

Per serving: 220 calories, 6g protein, 38g carbohydrates, 8g fat, 5g fiber, 0mg cholesterol, 550mg sodium, 600mg potassium.

Tempeh & Vegetable Curry Stew

INGREDIENTS

- 8 oz tempeh, cubed
- 2 medium carrots, sliced
- 1 bell pepper, diced
- 1 medium zucchini, diced
- 1 onion, finely chopped
- 2 cloves garlic, minced
- 1 can (14 oz) diced tomatoes
- 2 tablespoons curry powder
- 1 teaspoon turmeric
- 1/2 teaspoon cayenne pepper (optional, for extra heat)
- 3 cups vegetable broth
- 1 can (14 oz) coconut milk
- 2 tablespoons olive oil

Prep Time: 25 minutes

Cook Time: 4 hours

Serves: 4

DIRECTIONS

In a skillet, heat olive oil over medium heat. Add tempeh cubes and sear until golden brown on all sides. Transfer the tempeh to the slow cooker. In the same skillet, sauté the onions and garlic until translucent, then transfer to the slow cooker. Add carrots, bell pepper, zucchini, diced tomatoes, curry powder, turmeric, cayenne pepper (if using), and vegetable broth to the slow cooker. Cover and cook on low for 3.5 hours. Stir in coconut milk, season with salt and pepper, and continue cooking for another 30 minutes. Garnish with fresh cilantro before serving.

NUTRITIONAL INFORMATION

Per serving: 380 calories, 18g protein, 28g carbohydrates, 24g fat, 6g fiber, 0mg cholesterol, 750mg sodium, 800mg potassium.

Smoky Tomato & Lentil Soup

INGREDIENTS

- 1 cup dried green or brown lentils, rinsed and drained
- 1 large onion, diced
- 3 cloves garlic, minced
- 1 can (28 oz) crushed tomatoes
- 4 cups vegetable broth
- 2 carrots, diced
- 2 celery stalks, diced
- 1 teaspoon smoked paprika
- 1/2 teaspoon ground cumin
- 1/4 teaspoon cayenne pepper (optional)

Prep Time: 20 min

Cook Time: 6 hours

Serves: 4

DIRECTIONS

In a skillet, heat olive oil over medium heat. Sauté onions and garlic until translucent, then transfer to the slow cooker. Add lentils, crushed tomatoes, vegetable broth, carrots, celery, smoked paprika, cumin, and cayenne pepper (if using) to the slow cooker. Season with salt and pepper, then stir well to combine. Cover and cook on low for 5.5 hours. Check lentils for doneness; they should be tender but not mushy. Adjust seasoning if needed. Garnish with fresh parsley or basil before serving.

NUTRITIONAL INFORMATION

Per serving: 260 calories, 14g protein, 40g carbohydrates, 5g fat, 15g fiber, 0mg cholesterol, 850mg sodium, 750mg potassium.

Golden Turmeric & Cauliflower Chowder

INGREDIENTS

- 1 medium cauliflower head, chopped into florets
- 1 large onion, diced
- 2 cloves garlic, minced
- 4 cups vegetable broth
- 1 can (14 oz) coconut milk
- 1 tablespoon freshly grated turmeric (or 1 teaspoon ground turmeric)
- 1 teaspoon ground ginger
- Salt and pepper to taste
- 2 tablespoons olive oil
- Fresh cilantro or parsley for garnish
- Juice of half a lemon
- 1/4 cup cashews (optional, for creaminess)

Prep Time: 15 min

Cook Time: 4 hours

Serves: 4

DIRECTIONS

In a skillet, heat olive oil over medium heat. Sauté onions and garlic until translucent, then transfer to the slow cooker. Add cauliflower florets, vegetable broth, coconut milk, turmeric, ginger, and cashews (if using) to the slow cooker. Season with salt and pepper and stir well to combine. Cover and cook on low for 3.5 hours, or until the cauliflower is tender. Use an immersion blender to partially blend the soup, keeping some cauliflower chunks for texture. Stir in lemon juice and adjust seasoning if needed. Garnish with fresh cilantro or parsley before serving.

NUTRITIONAL INFORMATION

Per serving: 280 calories, 6g protein, 20g carbohydrates, 21g fat, 6g fiber, 0mg cholesterol, 850mg sodium, 550mg potassium.

Main Course Delights

Slow-Cooked Ratatouille Elegance

INGREDIENTS

- 1 large eggplant, diced into 1-inch cubes
- 2 zucchinis, sliced
- 1 red bell pepper, chopped
- 1 yellow bell pepper, chopped
- 1 medium onion, diced
- 3 cloves garlic, minced
- 2 cups diced tomatoes (canned or fresh)
- 1/4 cup extra-virgin olive oil
- 2 teaspoons dried basil
- 1 teaspoon dried thyme
- 1 tablespoon balsamic vinegar

Prep Time: 25 min

Cook Time: 6 hours

Serves: 4

DIRECTIONS

Layer the eggplant, zucchinis, bell peppers, and onion in the slow cooker. Add the garlic and diced tomatoes on top. Drizzle with olive oil and sprinkle with dried basil, thyme, salt, and pepper. Gently mix to combine. Cover and cook on low for 5.5 hours until the vegetables are tender and flavors melded. Before serving, stir in balsamic vinegar and adjust seasoning if needed. Garnish with fresh basil leaves.

NUTRITIONAL INFORMATION

Per serving: 200 calories, 4g protein, 28g carbohydrates, 10g fat, 8g fiber, 0mg cholesterol, 280mg sodium, 700mg potassium.

Teriyaki Tofu & Vegetable Casserole

INGREDIENTS

- 1 block (14 oz) firm tofu, pressed and cubed
- 1 broccoli head
- 2 carrots, thinly sliced
- 1 red bell pepper, chopped
- 1 yellow onion, thinly sliced
- 1/2 cup snap peas,
- 4 cloves garlic, minced
- 1/3 cup low-sodium teriyaki sauce
- 2 tablespoons tamari or soy sauce
- 1 tablespoon sesame oil, ground ginger
- 2 tablespoons maple syrup or agave nectar
- 2 tablespoons cornstarch mixed with 2 tablespoons cold water (to thicken)

Prep Time: 20 min

Cook Time: 4 hours

Serves: 4

DIRECTIONS

In a mixing bowl, whisk together teriyaki sauce, tamari, sesame oil, maple syrup, and ground ginger. Add the cubed tofu and marinate for at least 15 minutes. Place the marinated tofu and remaining marinade in the slow cooker. Add in broccoli, carrots, bell pepper, onion, snap peas, and garlic. Gently stir the ingredients to ensure they are well-coated with the sauce. Cover and cook on low for 3.5 hours. About 30 minutes before serving, stir in the cornstarch mixture to thicken the sauce. Garnish with sesame seeds and sliced green onions before serving.

NUTRITIONAL INFORMATION

Per serving: 230 calories, 14g protein, 30g carbohydrates, 7g fat, 5g fiber, 0mg cholesterol, 550mg sodium, 600mg potassium.

Barbecue Jackfruit Sliders

INGREDIENTS

- 2 cans (20 oz each) young green jackfruit in brine or water, drained and rinsed
- 1 1/2 cups barbecue sauce (ensure it's plant-based)
- 1/4 cup water
- 1 tablespoon olive oil
- 1 onion, thinly sliced
- 2 garlic cloves, minced
- 1 teaspoon smoked paprika
- 1/2 teaspoon cayenne pepper (optional for heat)
- Salt and black pepper, to taste
- 12 small slider buns
- Optional toppings: vegan coleslaw, pickles, onions

Prep Time: 15 min   Cook Time: 5 hours   Serves: 6

DIRECTIONS

In a bowl, shred the drained jackfruit with a fork or your hands until it resembles pulled meat. Heat olive oil in a pan over medium heat. Add onions and sauté until translucent, then add garlic and sauté for another 1-2 minutes. Transfer to the slow cooker. Add the shredded jackfruit, barbecue sauce, water, smoked paprika, cayenne pepper, salt, and black pepper to the slow cooker. Stir well to combine. Cover and cook on low for 4-5 hours, stirring occasionally, until the flavors meld and the jackfruit is tender. Serve the barbecue jackfruit on slider buns and top with your choice of toppings.

NUTRITIONAL INFORMATION

Per serving: 250 calories, 3g protein, 55g carbohydrates, 2g fat, 6g fiber, 0mg cholesterol, 500mg sodium, 300mg potassium.

Stuffed Bell Peppers with Quinoa & Veggies

INGREDIENTS

- 4 large bell peppers (any color), tops removed and seeds discarded
- 1 cup cooked quinoa
- 1 cup canned black beans, rinsed and drained
- 1 cup diced tomatoes
- 1 zucchini, diced
- 1 onion, finely chopped
- 2 cloves garlic, minced
- 1/2 cup corn kernels
- 1 teaspoon cumin, smoked paprika
- 2 cups vegetable broth
- 1/4 cup chopped fresh cilantro (for garnish, optional)

Prep Time: 25 min   Cook Time: 4 hours   Serves: 4

DIRECTIONS

In a large bowl, combine the cooked quinoa, black beans, diced tomatoes, zucchini, onion, garlic, corn, cumin, smoked paprika, salt, and pepper. Mix well to combine. Heat olive oil in a skillet over medium heat. Sauté the onion and garlic until translucent. Add zucchini and cook for another 2 minutes. Transfer the sautéed vegetables to the quinoa mixture and stir. Carefully stuff each bell pepper with the quinoa and vegetable mixture, pressing down to pack the filling. Place the stuffed bell peppers standing upright in the slow cooker. Pour the vegetable broth around the peppers. Cover and cook on low for 3-4 hours, or until the bell peppers are tender. Garnish with chopped cilantro before serving, if desired.

NUTRITIONAL INFORMATION

Per serving: 220 calories, 8g protein, 40g carbohydrates, 4g fat, 7g fiber, 0mg cholesterol, 350mg sodium, 650mg potassium.

Spaghetti Squash & Vegan Meatball Delight

INGREDIENTS

- 1 medium spaghetti squash, halved and seeds removed
- 1 cup store-bought or homemade vegan meatballs
- 2.5 cups marinara sauce (ensure it's vegan-friendly)
- 1 onion, finely chopped
- 2 cloves garlic, minced
- 1 tablespoon olive oil
- 1/4 cup nutritional yeast (optional for a cheesy flavor)
- 1 cup water

Prep Time: 30 min   Cook Time: 5 hours   Serves: 4

DIRECTIONS

Drizzle spaghetti squash with olive oil, salt, and pepper. Place cut sides down in a slow cooker. Sauté onion and garlic, add vegan meatballs, brown for 2 minutes per side. Pour marinara sauce over meatballs, simmer. Transfer mixture to slow cooker with squash. Add water, cover, cook on low for 5 hours. Fork to create squash "spaghetti". Serve meatballs and sauce over squash, garnish with basil, and sprinkle with nutritional yeast if desired.

NUTRITIONAL INFORMATION

Per serving: 280 calories, 15g protein, 40g carbohydrates, 8g fat, 7g fiber, 0mg cholesterol, 600mg sodium, 700mg potassium.

Moroccan Chickpea & Apricot Tagine

INGREDIENTS

- 2 cups cooked chickpeas (or 1 can, drained and rinsed)
- 1 cup dried apricots, halved
- 1 onion, finely chopped
- 2 cloves garlic, minced
- 1 red bell pepper, diced
- 1 carrot, sliced
- 1 can (14 oz) diced tomatoes, undrained
- 1/4 cup vegetable broth
- 2 teaspoons ground cumin
- 1 teaspoon ground coriander
- 1/2 teaspoon ground cinnamon
- 1/4 teaspoon cayenne pepper
- 2 tablespoons olive oil

Prep Time: 20 min   Cook Time: 6 hours   Serves: 4

DIRECTIONS

In a skillet over medium heat, sauté onion, garlic, red bell pepper, and carrot in olive oil until the onion becomes translucent. Add the cumin, coriander, cinnamon, cayenne pepper, salt, and black pepper to the skillet and stir for another minute until fragrant. Transfer the sautéed mixture to the slow cooker. Add chickpeas, apricots, diced tomatoes with their juice, and vegetable broth. Stir to combine. Cover and cook on low for 5-6 hours until the flavors meld and the vegetables are tender. Before serving, sprinkle with lemon zest and garnish with fresh cilantro.

NUTRITIONAL INFORMATION

Per serving: 340 calories, 10g protein, 58g carbohydrates, 9g fat, 11g fiber, 0mg cholesterol, 350mg sodium, 720mg potassium.

Eggplant & Mushroom Mousaka

INGREDIENTS

- 2 medium eggplants, sliced into 1/2-inch rounds
- 2 cups mushrooms, sliced
- 1 large onion, finely chopped
- 3 cloves garlic, minced
- 1 can (14 oz) diced tomatoes, undrained
- 1/4 cup red wine (optional)
- 2 tablespoons olive oil
- 1 teaspoon dried oregano
- 1 teaspoon dried basil
- 1/4 cup nutritional yeast (or vegan grated cheese)
- 1 cup unsweetened plant-based milk
- 2 tablespoons cornstarch

 Prep Time: 30 min

 Cook Time: 4 hours

 Serves: 4

DIRECTIONS

In a skillet, sauté the onion, garlic, and mushrooms in olive oil until tender. Add diced tomatoes, red wine (if using), oregano, basil, salt, and pepper. Cook for another 5 minutes, stirring occasionally. In the slow cooker, layer half of the eggplant slices, then spread half of the mushroom mixture over it. Repeat the layers. In a small saucepan, combine plant-based milk and cornstarch, stirring until smooth. Heat over medium heat, stirring constantly, until it thickens slightly. Pour this sauce over the layers in the slow cooker. Cover and cook on low for 4 hours, until the eggplant is tender. Before serving, sprinkle with nutritional yeast or vegan grated cheese.

NUTRITIONAL INFORMATION

Per serving: 220 calories, 7g protein, 30g carbohydrates, 8g fat, 9g fiber, 0mg cholesterol, 320mg sodium, 700mg potassium.

Tempeh Tikka Masala with Broccoli

INGREDIENTS

- 8 oz tempeh, cubed
- 2 cups broccoli florets
- 1 large onion, finely chopped
- 3 cloves garlic, minced
- 1-inch ginger, grated
- 1 can (14 oz) diced tomatoes, undrained
- 1 can (14 oz) coconut milk
- 2 tablespoons tomato paste
- 1 tablespoon garam masala
- 1 teaspoon turmeric
- 1 teaspoon paprika
- 1 teaspoon ground cumin
- 1/2 teaspoon chili powder

 Prep Time: 20 min

 Cook Time: 5 hours

 Serves: 4

DIRECTIONS

In a bowl, marinate tempeh cubes with garam masala, turmeric, paprika, cumin, and chili powder. Set aside for 10 minutes. In the slow cooker, combine the onion, garlic, ginger, diced tomatoes, tomato paste, and coconut milk. Mix well. Add the marinated tempeh and broccoli florets to the slow cooker, stirring to ensure they are well-coated with the mixture. Cover and cook on low for 5 hours. Season with salt to taste. Before serving, garnish with fresh cilantro.

NUTRITIONAL INFORMATION

Per serving: 370 calories, 18g protein, 25g carbohydrates, 25g fat, 8g fiber, 0mg cholesterol, 480mg sodium, 890mg potassium.

Smoky Vegan Sausage & Beans

INGREDIENTS

- 2 cups dried pinto beans, soaked overnight and drained
- 4 vegan sausages, sliced
- 1 large onion, chopped
- 3 cloves garlic, minced
- 1 can (14 oz) diced tomatoes with their juice
- 3 cups vegetable broth
- 1 teaspoon smoked paprika
- 1 teaspoon ground cumin
- 1/2 teaspoon chili powder (adjust to taste)
- 2 tablespoons chopped fresh parsley (for garnish)

 Prep Time: 15 min

 Cook Time: 6 hours

 Serves: 4

DIRECTIONS

In a pan over medium heat, add the olive oil and sauté the vegan sausage slices until they are slightly browned. Remove and set aside. In the same pan, sauté the onions and garlic until translucent. In the slow cooker, combine the soaked beans, browned sausages, sautéed onions and garlic, diced tomatoes, vegetable broth, smoked paprika, cumin, and chili powder. Cover and cook on low for 6 hours, or until the beans are tender. Season with salt and pepper. Serve in bowls, garnished with fresh parsley.

NUTRITIONAL INFORMATION

Per serving: 450 calories, 25g protein, 60g carbohydrates, 10g fat, 15g fiber, 0mg cholesterol, 720mg sodium, 1,200mg potassium.

Zesty Lemon & Artichoke Paella

INGREDIENTS

- 1.5 cups Arborio rice or short-grain rice
- 3.5 cups vegetable broth
- 1 cup marinated artichoke hearts, quartered
- 1 large onion, chopped
- 3 cloves garlic, minced
- 1 red bell pepper, diced
- 1 yellow bell pepper, diced
- 1/2 cup frozen green peas, thawed
- 1/4 cup fresh parsley, chopped
- 1/4 cup fresh cilantro, chopped
- 1 teaspoon smoked paprika
- 1/2 teaspoon saffron threads or turmeric

 Prep Time: 20 min

 Cook Time: 2.5 hours

 Serves: 4

DIRECTIONS

In a skillet over medium heat, heat the olive oil and sauté the onions, garlic, and bell peppers until the onions are translucent. Transfer the sautéed vegetables to the slow cooker. Add the rice, vegetable broth, lemon zest, lemon juice, artichoke hearts, smoked paprika, and saffron or turmeric. Stir to combine. Cover and cook on high for 2.5 hours, or until the rice is tender and has absorbed most of the liquid. About 15 minutes before serving, stir in the green peas, parsley, and cilantro. Season with salt and pepper. Serve hot, garnished with additional lemon zest or slices if desired.

NUTRITIONAL INFORMATION

Per serving: 410 calories, 9g protein, 72g carbohydrates, 10g fat, 6g fiber, 0mg cholesterol, 550mg sodium, 400mg potassium.

Butternut & Black Bean Enchilada Casserole

INGREDIENTS

- 2 cups butternut squash, peeled and diced into small cubes
- 1 can (15 oz.) black beans, drained and rinsed
- 2 cups enchilada sauce
- 1 medium onion, finely chopped
- 3 cloves garlic, minced
- 1 cup corn kernels
- 8 small corn tortillas
- 1 tsp ground cumin
- 1 tsp smoked paprika
- 1/4 cup fresh cilantro, chopped (for garnishing)
- 1/4 cup vegan cheese shreds (optional)

Prep Time: 25 min   Cook Time: 3 hours   Serves: 4

DIRECTIONS

In a large mixing bowl, combine the butternut squash, black beans, onion, garlic, corn, cumin, smoked paprika, and season with salt and pepper. Mix well.

In the slow cooker, spread a thin layer of enchilada sauce. Lay 2 tortillas at the bottom, slightly overlapping if necessary. Spread a portion of the butternut and black bean mixture on top, then a layer of enchilada sauce. Repeat layers, ending with enchilada sauce on top. Cover and cook on high for 3 hours or until the butternut squash is tender. If using, sprinkle the top with vegan cheese shreds in the last 20 minutes of cooking. Garnish with fresh cilantro before serving.

NUTRITIONAL INFORMATION

Per serving: 365 calories, 11g protein, 68g carbohydrates, 5g fat, 11g fiber, 0mg cholesterol, 800mg sodium, 800mg potassium.

Cauliflower & Chickpea Masala

INGREDIENTS

- 1 large cauliflower head, cut into florets
- 1 can (15 oz.) chickpeas, drained and rinsed
- 1 large onion, finely chopped
- 3 cloves garlic, minced
- 1 inch ginger, grated
- 1 can (14 oz.) diced tomatoes
- 1 can (14 oz.) coconut milk
- 2 tsp garam masala
- 1 tsp turmeric powder
- 1 tsp cumin seeds
- 1 tsp red chili powder

Prep Time: 20 min   Cook Time: 4 hours   Serves: 4

DIRECTIONS

In the slow cooker, add the coconut oil, onions, garlic, and ginger. Sauté until onions are translucent. Add the diced tomatoes, spices (garam masala, turmeric, cumin seeds, red chili powder), and salt. Mix well. Add the cauliflower florets, chickpeas, and coconut milk. Stir until everything is well combined. Cover and cook on low for 4 hours or until the cauliflower is tender and flavors melded. Garnish with fresh cilantro before serving. Can be served over rice or with flatbread.

NUTRITIONAL INFORMATION

Per serving: 320 calories, 10g protein, 40g carbohydrates, 16g fat, 10g fiber, 0mg cholesterol, 520mg sodium, 950mg potassium.

Savory Seitan Pot Roast

INGREDIENTS

- 1 lb seitan, cut into large chunks or a whole piece
- 3 large carrots, chopped into 1-inch pieces
- 3 medium potatoes, diced into 1-inch pieces
- 2 onions, sliced
- 3 cloves garlic, minced
- 2 cups vegetable broth
- 2 tbsp tomato paste, soy sauce or tamari
- 1 tsp dried rosemary, dried thyme
- 2 bay leaves

Prep Time: 25 min

Cook Time: 6 hours

Serves: 4

DIRECTIONS

In a skillet, heat the oil over medium heat. Add the seitan pieces and brown on all sides. Transfer to the slow cooker. To the slow cooker, add the carrots, potatoes, onions, and garlic. In a bowl, whisk together vegetable broth, tomato paste, soy sauce, rosemary, thyme, salt, and pepper. Pour this mixture over the ingredients in the slow cooker. Tuck the bay leaves into the mixture. Cover and cook on low for 6 hours or until vegetables are tender and flavors melded. Discard bay leaves before serving. Serve warm with vegan gravy or as is.

NUTRITIONAL INFORMATION

Per serving: 320 calories, 25g protein, 40g carbohydrates, 5g fat, 7g fiber, 0mg cholesterol, 680mg sodium, 980mg potassium.

Stuffed Portobello Mushrooms with Spinach & Rice

INGREDIENTS

- 4 large portobello mushrooms, stems removed and gills scraped
- 1 cup cooked brown rice
- 2 cups fresh spinach, roughly chopped
- 1 onion, finely diced
- 2 cloves garlic, minced
- 1/4 cup nutritional yeast (optional for a cheesy flavor)
- 1/2 cup vegetable broth
- 1 tsp dried oregano
- 1 tsp dried basil
- 1/4 cup vegan cheese shreds (optional)

Prep Time: 20 min

Cook Time: 4 hours

Serves: 4

DIRECTIONS

Sauté onions and garlic in 1 tbsp olive oil until translucent. Add spinach, cook until wilted, then cool. In a bowl, mix cooked rice, spinach mixture, nutritional yeast, oregano, basil, salt, and pepper. Brush portobello mushrooms with remaining olive oil, stuff with the rice-spinach mix. Pour vegetable broth into slow cooker, place mushrooms on top. Cook on low for 4 hours. Add vegan cheese shreds in the last 30 minutes if desired. Serve warm.

NUTRITIONAL INFORMATION

Per serving: 240 calories, 8g protein, 32g carbohydrates, 10g fat, 5g fiber, 0mg cholesterol, 250mg sodium, 480mg potassium.

Sweet Potato & Chickpea Coconut Curry

INGREDIENTS

- 2 large sweet potatoes, peeled and diced
- 1 can (15 oz) chickpeas, drained and rinsed
- 1 can (13.5 oz) full-fat coconut milk
- 1 large onion, finely diced
- 2 cloves garlic, minced
- 2 tsp curry powder
- 1 tsp turmeric
- 1 tsp cumin
- 1/2 tsp smoked paprika
- 1/4 tsp chili powder (adjust to taste)
- 1 tsp ginger, grated or minced
- 2 cups vegetable broth
- Salt to taste
- 1 handful of fresh cilantro, chopped (for garnish)
- 1 tbsp coconut oil or olive oil

Prep Time: 20 min

Cook Time: 6 hours

Serves: 4

DIRECTIONS

In a skillet, heat oil over medium heat. Add onions and garlic, sautéing until translucent. Add curry powder, turmeric, cumin, paprika, chili powder, and ginger, and sauté for an additional 2 minutes. Transfer the onion and spice mixture to the slow cooker. Add sweet potatoes, chickpeas, coconut milk, and vegetable broth. Stir well to combine. Set the slow cooker to low and cook for 6 hours, or until the sweet potatoes are tender. Taste and adjust salt as needed. Serve with fresh cilantro on top.

NUTRITIONAL INFORMATION

Per serving: 420 calories, 11g protein, 53g carbohydrates, 20g fat, 10g fiber, 0mg cholesterol, 530mg sodium, 720mg potassium.

Grains & Legume Magic

Creamy Coconut Millet Pudding

INGREDIENTS

- 11 cup millet, rinsed and drained
- 3 cups coconut milk (full fat)
- 1/4 cup coconut sugar (or adjust to taste)
- 1 tsp vanilla extract
- 1/4 tsp salt
- 1/2 tsp ground cinnamon
- 1/4 cup shredded unsweetened coconut
- 1/4 cup raisins or dried fruit of choice (optional)
- Zest of 1 lemon or orange (optional for added zing)

 Prep Time: 10 min

 Cook Time: 3 hours

 Serves: 4

DIRECTIONS

In the slow cooker, combine millet, coconut milk, coconut sugar, vanilla extract, salt, and cinnamon. Stir to ensure the millet is well submerged in the liquid. Set the slow cooker to low and cook for 3 hours, or until the millet is tender and has absorbed most of the coconut milk. Stir occasionally to prevent the millet from sticking to the bottom. About 10 minutes before serving, stir in the shredded coconut, raisins or dried fruit, and citrus zest if using. Serve warm, garnishing with additional coconut, fruit, or a sprinkle of cinnamon if desired.

NUTRITIONAL INFORMATION

Per serving: 450 calories, 9g protein, 60g carbohydrates, 20g fat, 5g fiber, 0mg cholesterol, 165mg sodium, 380mg potassium.

Rustic Chickpea & Rice Pilaf

INGREDIENTS

- 1 cup brown rice, rinsed and drained
- 1 can (15 oz) chickpeas, drained and rinsed
- 2 1/2 cups vegetable broth
- 1 medium onion, finely chopped
- 3 garlic cloves, minced
- 1/2 cup diced carrots
- 1/2 cup diced bell peppers (any color)
- 1 tsp ground cumin
- 1/2 tsp paprika
- 1/4 tsp turmeric
- 1/4 tsp black pepper

 Prep Time: 15 min

 Cook Time: 2.5 hours

 Serves: 4

DIRECTIONS

In the slow cooker, combine rice, chickpeas, vegetable broth, onion, garlic, carrots, and bell peppers. Drizzle olive oil over the mixture and then add cumin, paprika, turmeric, black pepper, and salt. Stir to combine all the ingredients well. Set the slow cooker on low and cook for 2.5 hours, or until rice is tender and has absorbed most of the liquid. Before serving, fluff the rice with a fork and garnish with fresh parsley or cilantro.

NUTRITIONAL INFORMATION

Per serving: 340 calories, 10g protein, 60g carbohydrates, 8g fat, 8g fiber, 0mg cholesterol, 750mg sodium, 410mg potassium.

Black Bean & Quinoa Fiesta Bowl

INGREDIENTS

- 1 cup quinoa, rinsed and drained
- 1 can (15 oz) black beans, drained and rinsed
- 2.5 cups vegetable broth
- 1 cup corn kernels (fresh, frozen, or canned)
- 1 red bell pepper, diced
- 1 green bell pepper, diced
- 1 medium onion, finely chopped
- 3 garlic cloves, minced
- 1 tsp ground cumin
- 1/2 tsp chili powder
- 1/4 tsp smoked paprika, black pepper

Prep Time: 20 minutes   Cook Time: 2.5 hours   Serves: 4

DIRECTIONS

In the slow cooker, combine quinoa, black beans, vegetable broth, corn, bell peppers, onion, and garlic. Drizzle olive oil over the mixture. Add cumin, chili powder, smoked paprika, salt, and black pepper, and stir to mix well. Set the slow cooker on low and cook for 2.5 hours, or until quinoa is tender and has absorbed the liquid. Before serving, fluff the quinoa mixture with a fork, and then drizzle with fresh lime juice and garnish with chopped cilantro.

NUTRITIONAL INFORMATION

Per serving: 350 calories, 12g protein, 58g carbohydrates, 8g fat, 11g fiber, 0mg cholesterol, 670mg sodium, 450mg potassium.

Lemon & Herb Farro Risotto

INGREDIENTS

- 1 cup farro, rinsed and drained
- 3 cups vegetable broth
- Zest and juice of 1 lemon
- 1 small onion, finely chopped
- 2 garlic cloves, minced
- 1 tbsp olive oil
- 1/4 cup nutritional yeast (or vegan Parmesan cheese, optional for creaminess)
- 1/4 cup chopped fresh basil
- 1/4 cup chopped fresh parsley
- 1/4 tsp red pepper flakes
- 2 tbsp vegan butter

Prep Time: 15 min   Cook Time: 2.5 hours   Serves: 4

DIRECTIONS

In the slow cooker, combine farro, vegetable broth, lemon zest, lemon juice, onion, and garlic. Drizzle olive oil over the mixture and stir. Set the slow cooker on low and cook for 2.5 hours, or until farro is tender and has absorbed most of the liquid. Stir in the nutritional yeast or vegan Parmesan cheese (if using), fresh herbs, salt, black pepper, red pepper flakes, and vegan butter. Cook for an additional 10-15 minutes, then serve.

NUTRITIONAL INFORMATION

Per serving: 280 calories, 8g protein, 48g carbohydrates, 7g fat, 10g fiber, 0mg cholesterol, 600mg sodium, 210mg potassium.

Spiced Lentils & Bulgar Ensemble

INGREDIENTS

- 1 cup dried green lentils, rinsed and drained
- 1/2 cup bulgar wheat
- 3 cups vegetable broth
- 1 medium onion, diced
- 2 garlic cloves, minced
- 1 tbsp olive oil
- 2 tsp ground cumin
- 1 tsp smoked paprika
- 1/2 tsp ground turmeric
- 1/2 tsp ground cinnamon
- 1/4 tsp cayenne pepper
- 1 bay leaf

 Prep Time: 20 min

 Cook Time: 3 hours

 Serves: 4

DIRECTIONS

In the slow cooker, combine lentils, bulgar wheat, vegetable broth, onion, and garlic. Drizzle with olive oil and stir in the spices: cumin, paprika, turmeric, cinnamon, cayenne pepper, bay leaf, salt, and black pepper. Set the slow cooker on low and cook for about 3 hours, or until lentils and bulgar are tender and have absorbed most of the liquid. Remove the bay leaf, adjust the seasoning if necessary, and serve the ensemble garnished with fresh parsley or cilantro.

NUTRITIONAL INFORMATION

Per serving: 280 calories, 16g protein, 48g carbohydrates, 4g fat, 14g fiber, 0mg cholesterol, 500mg sodium, 400mg potassium.

Moroccan Couscous & Vegetable Medley

INGREDIENTS

- 1 1/2 cups whole wheat couscous
- 2 cups vegetable broth
- 1 medium zucchini, sliced
- 1 red bell pepper, chopped
- 1 medium carrot, sliced
- 1/2 cup raisins or dried apricots, chopped
- 1 can (15 oz) chickpeas, drained and rinsed
- 2 tbsp olive oil
- 1 tsp ground cumin
- 1 tsp ground coriander
- 1/2 tsp ground cinnamon
- 1/4 tsp ground ginger

 Prep Time: 25 min

 Cook Time: 2 hours 30 minutes

 Serves: 4

DIRECTIONS:

In the slow cooker, combine zucchini, bell pepper, carrot, raisins/dried apricots, chickpeas, and spices. Drizzle with olive oil and mix to ensure the vegetables are well-coated. Pour the vegetable broth over the mixture, ensuring the vegetables are submerged. Cover and cook on low for 2 hours. After 2 hours, stir in the couscous, ensuring it's fully submerged in the liquid. Cover and cook for an additional 30 minutes or until the couscous is tender. Before serving, season with additional salt and pepper if desired, and garnish with fresh parsley and sliced almonds.

NUTRITIONAL INFORMATION

Per serving: 340 calories, 11g protein, 58g carbohydrates, 7g fat, 10g fiber, 0mg cholesterol, 400mg sodium, 500mg potassium.

Slow-Cooked Adzuki Beans & Barley

INGREDIENTS

- 1 cup adzuki beans, soaked overnight and drained
- 1/2 cup barley, rinsed and drained
- 4 cups vegetable broth
- 1 medium onion, chopped
- 2 garlic cloves, minced
- 1 carrot, diced
- 1 celery stalk, diced
- 1 bay leaf
- 1/2 tsp dried thyme
- Salt and pepper to taste
- Fresh parsley for garnish

Prep Time: 15 min

Cook Time: 6 hours

Serves: 4

DIRECTIONS

In your slow cooker, combine soaked adzuki beans, barley, onion, garlic, carrot, celery, bay leaf, and dried thyme. Pour in the vegetable broth ensuring that all ingredients are submerged. Cover and cook on low for 5-6 hours or until the beans and barley are tender. Once cooked, remove the bay leaf, season with salt and pepper to taste, and garnish with freshly chopped parsley before serving.

NUTRITIONAL INFORMATION

Per serving: 240 calories, 11g protein, 50g carbohydrates, 1g fat, 10g fiber, 0mg cholesterol, 550mg sodium, 650mg potassium.

Savory Mushroom & Buckwheat Groats

INGREDIENTS

- 1 cup buckwheat groats, rinsed and drained
- 2 1/2 cups vegetable broth
- 2 cups assorted mushrooms (e.g., shiitake, cremini, button), sliced
- 1 medium onion, finely chopped
- 2 garlic cloves, minced
- 2 tablespoons olive oil
- 1 teaspoon fresh rosemary, minced
- 1 teaspoon fresh thyme, minced
- Salt and pepper to taste
- Fresh parsley, chopped, for garnish

Prep Time: 20 min

Cook Time: 3 hours

Serves: 4

DIRECTIONS

In a pan over medium heat, add olive oil, onions, and garlic. Sauté until the onions are translucent. Add the mushrooms, rosemary, and thyme to the pan. Continue to cook until mushrooms are browned. Transfer the sautéed mixture into the slow cooker, adding buckwheat groats and vegetable broth. Stir well.
Cover and cook on low for 2.5 to 3 hours or until the buckwheat is tender and has absorbed most of the broth. Season with salt and pepper to taste, then garnish with freshly chopped parsley before serving.

NUTRITIONAL INFORMATION

Per serving: 230 calories, 8g protein, 38g carbohydrates, 6g fat, 5g fiber, 0mg cholesterol, 550mg sodium, 400mg potassium.

Fragrant Rosemary White Beans

INGREDIENTS

- 2 cups dried white beans (like cannellini or navy), soaked overnight and drained
- 4 cups vegetable broth
- 1 large onion, diced
- 3 cloves garlic, minced
- 2 sprigs fresh rosemary
- 1 bay leaf
- 2 tablespoons olive oil
- Zest and juice of 1 lemon
- Fresh parsley, chopped, for garnish

 Prep Time: 15 minutes

 Cook Time: 6 hours

 Serves: 4

DIRECTIONS

In the slow cooker, combine soaked beans, vegetable broth, onion, garlic, rosemary sprigs, bay leaf, and olive oil. Cover and cook on low for 5-6 hours or until beans are tender. Once cooked, remove the rosemary sprigs and bay leaf. Season with salt, pepper, lemon zest, and lemon juice. Stir well, garnish with fresh parsley, and serve warm.

NUTRITIONAL INFORMATION

Per serving: 310 calories, 18g protein, 48g carbohydrates, 7g fat, 12g fiber, 0mg cholesterol, 580mg sodium, 800mg potassium.

Golden Turmeric & Lentil Fusion

INGREDIENTS

- 1 cup dried green or brown lentils, rinsed and drained
- 3 cups vegetable broth
- 1 large onion, finely diced
- 3 cloves garlic, minced
- 1 tablespoon fresh ginger, grated
- 2 teaspoons ground turmeric
- 1 teaspoon ground cumin
- 1/2 teaspoon chili flakes (optional for a kick)
- 1 can (14 oz) diced tomatoes
- Juice of 1 lemon

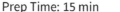 Prep Time: 15 min

 Cook Time: 4 hours

 Serves: 4

DIRECTIONS

In the slow cooker, combine lentils, vegetable broth, onion, garlic, ginger, turmeric, cumin, chili flakes (if using), and diced tomatoes. Drizzle in the coconut or olive oil, then stir to mix the ingredients well. Cover and set the slow cooker on low for 3.5 to 4 hours, or until lentils are soft and thoroughly cooked. Once done, season with salt and add the lemon juice. Stir well. Serve in bowls, garnishing with fresh cilantro.

NUTRITIONAL INFORMATION

Per serving: 280 calories, 15g protein, 40g carbohydrates, 7g fat, 16g fiber, 0mg cholesterol, 560mg sodium, 700mg potassium.

Hearty Three-Grain Risotto

INGREDIENTS

- 1/4 cup arborio rice
- 1/4 cup pearl barley
- 1/4 cup farro
- 4 cups vegetable broth
- 1 small onion, finely diced
- 2 cloves garlic, minced
- 1 cup mixed vegetables (e.g. bell peppers, zucchini, peas)
- 1 tablespoon olive oil
- 1/4 cup nutritional yeast or vegan parmesan
- 1/4 cup fresh parsley, chopped
- 1 tablespoon lemon zest

 Prep Time: 20 min

 Cook Time: 3 hours

 Serves: 4

DIRECTIONS

In the slow cooker, sauté onion and garlic in olive oil until translucent. Add the arborio rice, pearl barley, farro, and vegetable broth to the slow cooker. Stir well. Cover and cook on low for 2.5 to 3 hours or until grains are tender. Stir in the mixed vegetables, nutritional yeast or vegan parmesan, and season with salt and pepper. Cook for an additional 15 minutes or until vegetables are tender. Garnish with fresh parsley and lemon zest before serving.

NUTRITIONAL INFORMATION

Per serving: 290 calories, 10g protein, 55g carbohydrates, 5g fat, 8g fiber, 0mg cholesterol, 460mg sodium, 320mg potassium.

Chickpea & Wild Rice Soup

INGREDIENTS

- 1 cup dried chickpeas, soaked overnight and drained
- 1/2 cup wild rice, rinsed
- 1 large onion, diced
- 2 carrots, sliced
- 2 celery stalks, diced
- 3 garlic cloves, minced
- 6 cups vegetable broth
- 1 bay leaf
- 1 teaspoon dried thyme
- 1 teaspoon dried rosemary
- 2 cups kale, roughly chopped
- 1/4 cup fresh parsley, chopped (for garnish)

 Prep Time: 15 minutes

 Cook Time: 4 hours

 Serves: 4

DIRECTIONS

In the slow cooker, sauté onion, carrots, celery, and garlic in olive oil until translucent. Add chickpeas, wild rice, vegetable broth, bay leaf, thyme, rosemary, salt, and pepper. Stir to combine. Cover and cook on low for 3.5 hours. Stir in kale and continue cooking for another 30 minutes until chickpeas are tender and rice is fully cooked. Garnish with fresh parsley before serving.

NUTRITIONAL INFORMATION

Per serving: 320 calories, 14g protein, 60g carbohydrates, 4g fat, 10g fiber, 0mg cholesterol, 560mg sodium, 420mg potassium.

Red Bean & Millet Chili

INGREDIENTS

- 1 cup dried red beans, soaked overnight and drained
- 1/2 cup millet, rinsed
- 1 large onion, chopped
- 2 bell peppers (red and green), diced
- 3 garlic cloves, minced
- 1 can (28 ounces) diced tomatoes
- 4 cups vegetable broth
- 2 tablespoons chili powder
- 1 teaspoon ground cumin
- 1/2 teaspoon smoked paprika

 Prep Time: 20 min

 Cook Time: 6 hours

 Serves: 4

DIRECTIONS

In the slow cooker, sauté onion, bell peppers, and garlic in olive oil until translucent. Add soaked red beans, millet, diced tomatoes, vegetable broth, chili powder, cumin, smoked paprika, salt, and pepper. Stir well to combine. Cover and cook on low for 5.5 hours. Check the seasoning, adjust if necessary, and continue cooking for another 30 minutes. Serve hot with optional toppings if desired.

NUTRITIONAL INFORMATION

Per serving: 360 calories, 15g protein, 65g carbohydrates, 4.5g fat, 13g fiber, 0mg cholesterol, 700mg sodium, 800mg potassium.

Cumin & Spinach Lentil Stew

INGREDIENTS

- 1 cup dried green lentils, rinsed and drained
- 4 cups fresh spinach, roughly chopped
- 1 large onion, diced
- 3 garlic cloves, minced
- 1 can (14 ounces) diced tomatoes
- 4 cups vegetable broth
- 2 teaspoons ground cumin
- 1/2 teaspoon smoked paprika
- 1/4 teaspoon cayenne pepper (optional for heat)
- Salt and pepper to taste
- 2 tablespoons olive oil
- Juice of 1 lemon

 Prep Time: 15 min

 Cook Time: 6 hours

 Serves: 4

DIRECTIONS

In the slow cooker, sauté onion and garlic in olive oil until translucent. Add lentils, chopped spinach, diced tomatoes, vegetable broth, cumin, smoked paprika, cayenne (if using), salt, and pepper. Stir to combine. Cover and cook on low for 5.5 hours. Before serving, stir in fresh lemon juice and adjust seasoning if necessary. Serve hot with your favorite crusty bread or side dish.

NUTRITIONAL INFORMATION

Per serving: 330 calories, 18g protein, 52g carbohydrates, 6g fat, 14g fiber, 0mg cholesterol, 680mg sodium, 750mg potassium.

Smoky Black-Eyed Peas & Rice

INGREDIENTS

- 1 cup dried black-eyed peas, soaked overnight and drained
- 1 cup long-grain brown rice
- 1 onion, diced
- 3 garlic cloves, minced
- 1 smoked bell pepper (or regular), diced
- 4 cups vegetable broth
- 1 teaspoon smoked paprika
- 1/2 teaspoon ground cumin
- 1/4 teaspoon cayenne pepper (optional for heat)
- Salt and pepper to taste
- 2 tablespoons olive oil
- Fresh parsley or cilantro for garnish

Prep Time: 20 min

Cook Time: 6 hours

Serves: 4

DIRECTIONS

In your slow cooker, add olive oil, onion, garlic, and bell pepper. Stir until well combined. Add the drained black-eyed peas, brown rice, vegetable broth, smoked paprika, cumin, cayenne (if using), salt, and pepper. Cover and cook on low for 5-6 hours, or until the rice is tender and the peas are cooked through.

Before serving, adjust seasoning if necessary, and garnish with freshly chopped parsley or cilantro. Serve hot and enjoy the smoky flavor with your favorite greens.

NUTRITIONAL INFORMATION

Per serving: 340 calories, 16g protein, 60g carbohydrates, 7g fat, 9g fiber, 0mg cholesterol, 750mg sodium, 620mg potassium.

Pasta &
Noodles

Creamy Vegan Alfredo with Fettuccine

INGREDIENTS

- 12 oz. fettuccine (whole wheat or gluten-free for healthier options)
- 1 cup raw cashews, soaked for 4 hours and drained
- 3 cups vegetable broth
- 4 garlic cloves, minced
- 1 small onion, chopped
- 1 tablespoon olive oil
- 1/2 cup unsweetened almond milk
- 2 tablespoons nutritional yeast
- 1/4 teaspoon black pepper
- 1 tablespoon lemon juice

Prep Time: 15 minutes

Cook Time: 3 hours

Serves: 4

DIRECTIONS

In the slow cooker, add olive oil, minced garlic, and chopped onion. Stir to coat. In a blender, combine the soaked and drained cashews, almond milk, nutritional yeast, salt, pepper, and lemon juice. Blend until smooth and creamy. Pour the cashew mixture into the slow cooker along with the vegetable broth, stirring to combine. Break the fettuccine in half and add to the slow cooker, ensuring they are submerged in the liquid. Cook on low for 2-3 hours or until pasta is al dente. Before serving, adjust seasoning if needed, and garnish with fresh parsley and optional red pepper flakes.

NUTRITIONAL INFORMATION

Per serving: 490 calories, 18g protein, 72g carbohydrates, 15g fat, 5g fiber, 0mg cholesterol, 650mg sodium, 450mg potassium.

Thai Peanut & Vegetable Noodle Pot

INGREDIENTS

- 8 oz. rice noodles
- 3 cups mixed vegetables
- 1 can (14 oz.) coconut milk
- 1/3 cup peanut butter, smooth
- 3 tablespoons soy sauce (or tamari for gluten-free)
- 2 tablespoons lime juice
- 2 garlic cloves, minced
- 1-inch piece ginger, minced
- 1 tablespoon maple syrup or agave nectar
- 2 green onions, sliced for garnish
- 1/4 cup chopped roasted peanuts, for garnish

Prep Time: 20 min

Cook Time: 3 houri

Serves: 4

DIRECTIONS

In the slow cooker, combine coconut milk, peanut butter, soy sauce, lime juice, garlic, ginger, maple syrup, and red pepper flakes. Stir until smooth. Add the mixed vegetables to the slow cooker, ensuring they are coated in the sauce. Cook on low for 2.5 hours. Add the rice noodles and stir gently. Continue to cook for another 30 minutes or until noodles are tender. Serve in bowls, garnishing with green onions, cilantro, and roasted peanuts.

NUTRITIONAL INFORMATION

Per serving: 550 calories, 14g protein, 75g carbohydrates, 25g fat, 6g fiber, 0mg cholesterol, 800mg sodium, 600mg potassium.

Rustic Veggie Lasagna Layers

INGREDIENTS

- 9 lasagna noodles, uncooked
- 1 jar (24 oz.) marinara sauce (preferably with no added sugar)
- 1 zucchini, thinly sliced
- 1 yellow bell pepper, thinly sliced
- 1 cup mushrooms, thinly sliced
- 1 cup fresh spinach
- 2 cups vegan ricotta cheese (store-bought or homemade)
- 1 cup vegan mozzarella cheese, shredded

Prep Time: 30 minutes   Cook Time: 4 houri   Serves: 4

DIRECTIONS

In a bowl, mix vegan ricotta cheese, vegan mozzarella cheese, fresh basil, and nutritional yeast. Set aside. Drizzle olive oil at the base of the slow cooker. Layer 3 lasagna noodles at the bottom. Spread a third of the marinara sauce over the noodles, then a third of the vegetable mixture, and top with a third of the cheese mixture. Season with salt and pepper. Repeat layering two more times. Cover and cook on low for 4 hours, or until the noodles are tender. Before serving, let it rest for 10 minutes. Garnish with fresh parsley.

NUTRITIONAL INFORMATION

Per serving: 480 calories, 18g protein, 65g carbohydrates, 15g fat, 9g fiber, 0mg cholesterol, 820mg sodium, 600mg potassium.

Slow-Cooked Vegetable Lo Mein

INGREDIENTS

- 8 oz lo mein noodles (or spaghetti if unavailable)
- 1 cup julienned bell peppers, julienned carrots, sliced mushrooms, snap peas or snow peas, halved
- 1/2 cup sliced green onions
- 3 cloves garlic, minced
- 4 tablespoons soy sauce
- 2 tablespoons hoisin sauce
- 1 tablespoon agave nectar or maple syrup, sesame oil
- 1/2 cup vegetable broth
- 1 tablespoon fresh ginger, grated
- 1 tablespoon cornstarch mixed with 2 tablespoons water

Prep Time: 20 min   Cook Time: 2 hours 30 minutes   Serves: 4

DIRECTIONS

In a bowl, whisk together soy sauce, hoisin sauce, agave nectar, sesame oil, ginger, and vegetable broth. Set aside. Add julienned bell peppers, carrots, mushrooms, snap peas, green onions, and minced garlic into the slow cooker. Pour the sauce mixture over the vegetables. Stir to coat. Cover and cook on low for 2 hours. After 2 hours, stir in the cornstarch mixture and add the lo mein noodles, ensuring they are submerged in the liquid. Continue cooking for another 20-30 minutes or until noodles are tender. Serve hot, garnished with sesame seeds and red pepper flakes.

NUTRITIONAL INFORMATION

Per serving: 350 calories, 9g protein, 62g carbohydrates, 7g fat, 5g fiber, 0mg cholesterol, 780mg sodium, 420mg potassium.

Spaghetti with Vegan Bolognese Sauce

INGREDIENTS

- 8 oz whole wheat spaghetti
- 2 cups (about 12 oz) meatless ground "meat"
- 1 large onion, diced
- 2 cloves garlic, minced
- 1 large carrot, diced
- 1 bell pepper, diced
- 1 zucchini, diced
- 1 can (28 oz) crushed tomatoes
- 1/4 cup tomato paste
- 2 teaspoons dried basil
- 1 teaspoon dried oregano
- 1/2 teaspoon dried thyme
- 1 bay leaf
- 1/2 cup red wine (optional)

 Prep Time: 15 min

 Cook Time: 4 houri

 Serves: 4

DIRECTIONS

In the slow cooker, heat olive oil and add diced onion, garlic, carrot, bell pepper, and zucchini. Sauté for a few minutes until softened. Add meatless ground "meat", crushed tomatoes, tomato paste, basil, oregano, thyme, bay leaf, and red wine if using. Stir to combine. Season with salt and pepper, cover, and cook on low for 3.5 hours. About 20 minutes before serving, prepare the spaghetti according to package instructions. Drain and set aside. Serve the vegan bolognese sauce over spaghetti, garnished with fresh parsley.

NUTRITIONAL INFORMATION

Per serving: 480 calories, 22g protein, 75g carbohydrates, 10g fat, 13g fiber, 0mg cholesterol, 680mg sodium, 900mg potassium.

Zucchini Noodle & Mushroom Stroganoff

INGREDIENTS

- 4 medium zucchinis, spiralized into noodles
- 16 oz (about 2 cups) fresh mushrooms, sliced
- 1 large onion, diced
- 2 cloves garlic, minced
- 1.5 cups cashew cream
- 2 tablespoons tamari or soy sauce
- 1 tablespoon olive oil
- 1 tablespoon nutritional yeast (optional for a cheesy flavor)
- 1/4 cup vegetable broth
- 2 teaspoons smoked paprika

 Prep Time: 20 min

 Cook Time: 3 houri

 Serves: 4

DIRECTIONS

In the slow cooker, heat olive oil and add diced onion, garlic, and mushrooms. Sauté until the mushrooms release their juices. Add vegetable broth, tamari or soy sauce, smoked paprika, and nutritional yeast if using. Stir well. Pour in the cashew cream, stirring to combine. Adjust seasoning with salt and pepper. Cover and cook on low for 2.5 hours. Just before serving, add spiralized zucchini noodles, mixing gently. Cover and let it cook for an additional 15-20 minutes until the zoodles are tender. Garnish with fresh parsley or dill before serving.

NUTRITIONAL INFORMATION

Per serving: 290 calories, 9g protein, 25g carbohydrates, 20g fat, 6g fiber, 0mg cholesterol, 540mg sodium, 980mg potassium.

Butternut Squash & Sage Pasta Casserole

INGREDIENTS

- 3 cups diced butternut squash
- 12 oz (about 3 cups) whole grain or gluten-free pasta (uncooked)
- 2.5 cups unsweetened almond milk
- 1/4 cup nutritional yeast
- 1 onion, finely chopped
- 3 cloves garlic, minced
- 10 fresh sage leaves, chopped
- 2 tablespoons olive oil
- 1 teaspoon smoked paprika
- 1/2 cup vegan cheese shreds (optional)
- 1/4 cup bread crumbs

Prep Time: 30 min   Cook Time: 4 houri   Serves: 4

DIRECTIONS

In a pan, sauté onions and garlic in olive oil until translucent. Add chopped sage leaves and sauté for another 2 minutes. Transfer the onion-garlic-sage mix to the slow cooker. Add diced butternut squash, almond milk, nutritional yeast, smoked paprika, salt, and pepper. Mix well. Gently fold in the uncooked pasta, ensuring it's well coated with the sauce. If using, sprinkle vegan cheese shreds on top. Cover and cook on low for 3.5 hours. 15 minutes before serving, sprinkle bread crumbs on top and continue to cook until they're golden. Let the casserole sit for about 10 minutes before serving. It will thicken as it cools.

NUTRITIONAL INFORMATION

Per serving: 410 calories, 12g protein, 75g carbohydrates, 8g fat, 8g fiber, 0mg cholesterol, 220mg sodium, 650mg potassium.

Vegetable Pad Thai with Tofu

INGREDIENTS

- 8 oz rice noodles
- 14 oz firm tofu, drained, pressed, and cubed
- 2 cups julienned carrots
- 1 red bell pepper
- 2 cups snap peas, halved
- 4 green onions, sliced
- 3 cloves garlic, minced
- 1/4 cup tamari or soy sauce
- 3 tablespoons brown sugar
- 2 tablespoons tamarind paste
- 1/2 teaspoon red pepper flakes (adjust to taste)
- 2 tablespoons vegetable oil

Prep Time: 25 min   Cook Time: 2 hours   Serves: 4

DIRECTIONS

In a pan, heat the vegetable oil over medium-high heat. Add tofu cubes and fry until golden brown on all sides. Remove and set aside. In the slow cooker, whisk together tamari, brown sugar, lime juice, tamarind paste, and red pepper flakes. Add the fried tofu, carrots, bell pepper, snap peas, green onions, and garlic to the slow cooker, mixing gently to ensure all ingredients are coated with the sauce. Cover and cook on low for 1.5 hours. Add the rice noodles and gently stir to combine. Cover again and cook for an additional 30 minutes or until noodles are tender. Serve hot, garnished with chopped peanuts and cilantro.

NUTRITIONAL INFORMATION

Per serving: 465 calories, 18g protein, 65g carbohydrates, 15g fat, 5g fiber, 0mg cholesterol, 720mg sodium, 620mg potassium.

Lemon & Artichoke Orzo Delight

INGREDIENTS

- 1 1/2 cups orzo pasta
- 3 cups vegetable broth
- 1 cup canned artichoke hearts, drained and chopped
- 3 cloves garlic, minced
- 1/4 cup fresh parsley, chopped
- 1/2 cup vegan Parmesan cheese (optional)
- 1/4 cup chopped sun-dried tomatoes
- 1 tablespoon capers
- 1/2 teaspoon red pepper flakes

Prep Time: 15 min

Cook Time: 2 hours 30 minutes

Serves: 4

DIRECTIONS

In the slow cooker, combine vegetable broth, orzo, artichoke hearts, lemon zest, lemon juice, garlic, sun-dried tomatoes, capers, olive oil, salt, pepper, and red pepper flakes. Stir to mix well. Cover and cook on low for 2 hours, or until the orzo is tender and has absorbed most of the liquid. Once cooked, stir in the chopped parsley and vegan Parmesan cheese until well combined. Taste and adjust seasoning if necessary. Serve hot.

NUTRITIONAL INFORMATION

Per serving: 370 calories, 11g protein, 60g carbohydrates, 10g fat, 5g fiber, 0mg cholesterol, 580mg sodium, 420mg potassium.

Spinach & Vegan Ricotta Stuffed Shells

INGREDIENTS

- 18 jumbo pasta shells
- 2 cups vegan ricotta cheese (store-bought or homemade)
- 2 cups fresh spinach, chopped
- 3 cups vegan marinara sauce
- 1/4 cup vegan mozzarella cheese, shredded
- 2 cloves garlic, minced
- 1 tablespoon olive oil
- 1 teaspoon dried oregano

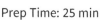

Prep Time: 25 min

Cook Time: 3 hours

Serves: 4

DIRECTIONS

Undercook jumbo pasta shells by 2 minutes. In a bowl, combine vegan ricotta, chopped spinach, garlic, oregano, salt, and pepper. Mix well. Spread 1 cup marinara sauce in slow cooker. Stuff shells with the spinach-ricotta mix, place seam-side down. Pour remaining marinara sauce over shells. Drizzle with olive oil, sprinkle with vegan mozzarella. Cover, cook on low for 3 hours. Serve hot, garnish with fresh basil if desired.

NUTRITIONAL INFORMATION

Per serving: 380 calories, 15g protein, 55g carbohydrates, 12g fat, 6g fiber, 0mg cholesterol, 680mg sodium, 500mg potassium.

Pesto Penne with Sundried Tomatoes

INGREDIENTS

- 2 cups penne pasta
- 1 cup vegan basil pesto (store-bought or homemade)
- 1/2 cup sundried tomatoes, chopped
- 3 cups vegetable broth
- 1 cup vegan parmesan cheese, grated
- 1/4 cup fresh basil leaves, chopped (for garnish)
- 2 cloves garlic, minced
- 1 tablespoon olive oil

Prep Time: 15 min

Cook Time: 2 hours 30 minutes

Serves: 4

DIRECTIONS

In the slow cooker, combine penne pasta, vegan pesto, sundried tomatoes, garlic, olive oil, and vegetable broth. Mix well to ensure pasta is submerged in the liquid. Cover and cook on low for 2 hours 30 minutes, or until the pasta is al dente. Stir occasionally to prevent sticking. Once cooked, stir in half of the vegan parmesan cheese. Season with salt, pepper, and chili flakes if using. Serve hot, garnished with the remaining vegan parmesan cheese and fresh basil.

NUTRITIONAL INFORMATION

Per serving: 430 calories, 14g protein, 62g carbohydrates, 14g fat, 5g fiber, 0mg cholesterol, 740mg sodium, 450mg potassium..

Cajun Spiced Linguine with Okra

INGREDIENTS

- 2 cups linguine pasta
- 2 cups fresh okra, sliced
- 1 medium red bell pepper, diced
- 1 medium onion, finely chopped
- 2 cloves garlic, minced
- 2 tablespoons olive oil
- 2 cups vegetable broth
- 1 tablespoon Cajun spice mix
- 1 teaspoon smoked paprika
- 2 green onions, thinly sliced (for garnish)
- 1 lemon, zested and juiced

Prep Time: 20 min

Cook Time: 3 hours

Serves: 4

DIRECTIONS

In your slow cooker, add olive oil, garlic, onion, red bell pepper, and okra. Stir to mix. Pour in vegetable broth, followed by the linguine. Ensure that the linguine is submerged in the broth. Add the Cajun spice mix, smoked paprika, salt, pepper, lemon zest, and lemon juice. Gently mix until combined. Cover and cook on low for 3 hours, stirring occasionally to prevent sticking. Once cooked, adjust seasonings if needed. Serve hot, garnished with green onions and parsley.

NUTRITIONAL INFORMATION

Per serving: 370 calories, 12g protein, 58g carbohydrates, 10g fat, 6g fiber, 0mg cholesterol, 650mg sodium, 420mg potassium.

Vegan Mac and Cheese Extravaganza

INGREDIENTS

- 2 cups elbow macaroni (preferably whole grain)
- 2.5 cups unsweetened almond milk or other plant-based milk
- 1 cup raw cashews, soaked for 2 hours or boiled for 10 minutes and drained
- 1/4 cup nutritional yeast
- 1 tablespoon olive oil
- 1 teaspoon garlic powder
- 1 teaspoon onion powder
- 1/2 teaspoon turmeric (for color)
- 1/4 teaspoon smoked paprika

Prep Time: 15 min

Cook Time: 2 hours 30 minutes

Serves: 4

DIRECTIONS

In a blender, combine soaked cashews, almond milk, nutritional yeast, garlic powder, onion powder, turmeric, smoked paprika, olive oil, salt, and pepper. Blend until smooth. Pour the blended mixture into the slow cooker and add the uncooked macaroni. Stir to combine. Cover and cook on low for 2 hours, stirring occasionally. After 2 hours, check the pasta for doneness. If desired, stir in vegan cheddar cheese shreds until melted and combined. Serve hot, garnished with fresh parsley.

NUTRITIONAL INFORMATION

Per serving: 450 calories, 15g protein, 65g carbohydrates, 15g fat, 7g fiber, 0mg cholesterol, 200mg sodium, 320mg potassium.

Chickpea Pasta & Vegetable Minestrone

INGREDIENTS

- 1 cup chickpea pasta (uncooked)
- 1 can (15 oz.) chickpeas, drained and rinsed
- 1 large carrot, diced
- 1 celery stalk, diced
- 1 zucchini, onion
- 3 cloves garlic, minced
- 1 can (14.5 oz.) diced tomatoes, undrained
- 4 cups vegetable broth
- 1 teaspoon dried oregano, basil
- 1 bay leaf
- 2 cups spinach or kale, roughly chopped

Prep Time: 20 min

Cook Time: 6 hours

Serves: 4

DIRECTIONS

In the slow cooker, combine onion, garlic, carrot, celery, zucchini, chickpeas, diced tomatoes, vegetable broth, oregano, basil, bay leaf, olive oil, salt, and pepper. Cover and cook on low for 5 hours. After 5 hours, add the chickpea pasta and spinach or kale. Stir well and continue cooking for another hour or until the pasta is tender. Once cooked, remove the bay leaf. Adjust seasoning with salt and pepper if necessary. Serve hot and enjoy!

NUTRITIONAL INFORMATION

Per serving: 420 calories, 18g protein, 68g carbohydrates, 10g fat, 12g fiber, 0mg cholesterol, 560mg sodium, 740mg potassium.

Seitan & Vegetable Noodle Soup

INGREDIENTS

- 8 oz. seitan, sliced into bite-sized pieces
- 6 cups vegetable broth
- 2 medium carrots, sliced
- 2 celery stalks, sliced
- 1 medium onion, chopped
- 3 garlic cloves, minced
- 4 oz. whole grain noodles (e.g., spaghetti, broken into smaller pieces)
- 2 bay leaves
- 1 tsp dried thyme
- 1 tsp dried rosemary
- Salt and pepper, to taste
- 1 tablespoon olive oil
- 2 cups spinach, roughly chopped
- 1 tablespoon soy sauce or tamari
- 2 green onions, sliced for garnish

Prep Time: 15 min

Cook Time: 4 hours

Serves: 4

DIRECTIONS

In the slow cooker, combine seitan, carrots, celery, onion, garlic, bay leaves, thyme, rosemary, olive oil, soy sauce, and vegetable broth. Cover and set to cook on low for 3 hours. After 3 hours, add the noodles and spinach to the pot. Stir well and continue cooking for another hour, or until noodles are tender. Once cooked, remove the bay leaves. Adjust seasoning with salt, pepper, and additional soy sauce if needed. Serve in bowls, garnished with sliced green onions.

NUTRITIONAL INFORMATION

Per serving: 320 calories, 20g protein, 45g carbohydrates, 5g fat, 7g fiber, 0mg cholesterol, 900mg sodium, 620mg potassium.

Side Dishes
& Accents

Balsamic Glazed Brussels Sprouts

INGREDIENTS

- 1.5 lbs Brussels sprouts, trimmed and halved
- 1/4 cup balsamic vinegar
- 2 tablespoons olive oil
- 2 tablespoons maple syrup
- 3 garlic cloves, minced
- Salt and pepper, to taste
- 1/4 cup water
- 1 tablespoon fresh rosemary, finely chopped
- 1 tablespoon fresh thyme, finely chopped
- 1/4 cup crushed walnuts for garnish (optional)

 Prep Time: 10 min

 Cook Time: 3 hours

 Serves: 4

DIRECTIONS

In a mixing bowl, whisk together balsamic vinegar, olive oil, maple syrup, garlic, salt, and pepper. Place Brussels sprouts in the slow cooker and pour the balsamic mixture over them. Add water, rosemary, and thyme. Gently stir to coat all the Brussels sprouts. Cover and set to cook on low for 3 hours, or until Brussels sprouts are tender and well-glazed. Prior to serving, toss with crushed walnuts if desired for added texture. Serve hot, ensuring every portion has a generous amount of the balsamic glaze.

NUTRITIONAL INFORMATION

Per serving: 190 calories, 6g protein, 28g carbohydrates, 7g fat, 5g fiber, 0mg cholesterol, 40mg sodium, 600mg potassium.

Garlic & Rosemary Roasted Potatoes

INGREDIENTS

- 2 lbs red or gold potatoes, washed and quartered
- 4 garlic cloves, minced
- 2 tablespoons fresh rosemary, finely chopped
- 3 tablespoons olive oil
- Salt and pepper, to taste
- 1/4 cup vegetable broth or water
- 1 tablespoon fresh parsley, chopped (optional for garnish)

 Prep Time: 15 min

 Cook Time: 4 hours

 Serves: 4

DIRECTIONS

In a large mixing bowl, combine the quartered potatoes, minced garlic, chopped rosemary, olive oil, salt, and pepper. Toss well until all potatoes are coated. Transfer the coated potatoes to the slow cooker and pour in the vegetable broth or water. Cover and cook on high for 4 hours, or until potatoes are tender and slightly crispy on the edges. Once done, transfer to a serving dish and garnish with fresh parsley if desired.

NUTRITIONAL INFORMATION

Per serving: 210 calories, 4g protein, 36g carbohydrates, 7g fat, 3g fiber, 0mg cholesterol, 70mg sodium, 950mg potassium.

Savory Vegan Stuffing with Cranberries

INGREDIENTS

- 8 cups cubed whole grain bread, dried overnight
- 1 cup fresh cranberries
- 1 onion, finely chopped
- 3 celery stalks, chopped
- 2 garlic cloves, minced
- 1/4 cup fresh parsley, chopped
- 1 tablespoon fresh rosemary, finely chopped
- 1 tablespoon fresh sage, chopped
- 2 cups vegetable broth
- 2 tablespoons olive oil
- Salt and pepper, to taste

 Prep Time: 20 min

 Cook Time: 4 hour

 Serves: 6

DIRECTIONS

In a large bowl, combine the dried bread cubes, cranberries, onion, celery, garlic, parsley, rosemary, and sage. In a separate bowl, mix the vegetable broth with the olive oil, salt, and pepper. Pour this mixture over the bread and stir to combine. Transfer the mixture to the slow cooker, spreading it out evenly. Cover and cook on low for 4 hours, occasionally stirring to ensure even cooking.

Once cooked, the stuffing should be moist with crispy edges. Adjust salt and pepper to taste before serving.

NUTRITIONAL INFORMATION

Per serving: 230 calories, 6g protein, 40g carbohydrates, 6g fat, 5g fiber, 0mg cholesterol, 550mg sodium, 320mg potassium.

Lemon & Dill Steamed Green Beans

INGREDIENTS

- 1 lb fresh green beans, trimmed
- Zest and juice of 1 lemon
- 2 tablespoons fresh dill, finely chopped
- 1/2 cup vegetable broth
- 2 garlic cloves, minced
- Salt and pepper, to taste
- 1 tablespoon olive oil (optional, for drizzling)

 Prep Time: 10 min

 Cook Time: 2 hours

 Serves: 4

DIRECTIONS

In the slow cooker, combine green beans, lemon zest, lemon juice, dill, vegetable broth, and minced garlic. Toss to ensure the green beans are well-coated. Cover and set the slow cooker to low heat. Cook for 2 hours, or until the green beans are tender but still vibrant in color. Once done, season with salt and pepper and give it a good stir. Serve the green beans in a dish, optionally drizzling with a bit of olive oil for added richness.

NUTRITIONAL INFORMATION

Per serving: 60 calories, 2g protein, 12g carbohydrates, 1g fat, 4g fiber, 0mg cholesterol, 150mg sodium, 250mg potassium.

Curried Cauliflower & Peas

INGREDIENTS

- 1 large cauliflower, cut into florets
- 1 cup green peas (frozen or fresh)
- 1 can (14 oz.) coconut milk
- 2 tablespoons curry powder
- 1 teaspoon turmeric
- 1 teaspoon cumin
- 1/2 teaspoon chili powder (adjust to preference)
- 2 garlic cloves, minced
- 1 medium onion, finely chopped
- Salt and pepper, to taste
- Fresh cilantro, for garnish (optional)
- 1 tablespoon olive oil

Prep Time: 15 min

Cook Time: 4 hours

Serves: 4

DIRECTIONS

In the slow cooker, combine cauliflower florets, peas, coconut milk, curry powder, turmeric, cumin, chili powder, minced garlic, and chopped onion. Mix well to ensure all ingredients are coated with the spices and coconut milk. Drizzle with olive oil and season with salt and pepper. Cover and set the slow cooker on low heat for 4 hours. The cauliflower should be tender but not mushy. Once cooked, adjust seasoning if necessary and garnish with fresh cilantro before serving.

NUTRITIONAL INFORMATION

Per serving: 220 calories, 7g protein, 27g carbohydrates, 12g fat, 8g fiber, 0mg cholesterol, 180mg sodium, 650mg potassium.

Smoky Maple Roasted Carrots

INGREDIENTS

- 1 lb. fresh carrots, peeled and halved lengthwise
- 3 tablespoons maple syrup
- 1 tablespoon olive oil
- 1 teaspoon smoked paprika
- 1/2 teaspoon salt (or to taste)
- 1/4 teaspoon black pepper
- 2 cloves garlic, minced
- 1 tablespoon fresh rosemary, finely chopped (optional)

Prep Time: 10 min

Cook Time: 3 hours

Serves: 4

DIRECTIONS

In a large mixing bowl, combine maple syrup, olive oil, smoked paprika, salt, pepper, minced garlic, and rosemary (if using). Stir to combine. Add the halved carrots to the bowl and toss to coat them evenly with the mixture. Transfer the coated carrots to the slow cooker. Cover and set the slow cooker on low heat for 3 hours. Check occasionally to ensure the carrots are tender and not overcooked.

NUTRITIONAL INFORMATION

Per serving: 130 calories, 2g protein, 27g carbohydrates, 4g fat, 4g fiber, 0mg cholesterol, 320mg sodium, 450mg potassium.

Sweet Corn & Basil Succotash

INGREDIENTS

- 3 cups fresh corn kernels (from about 4 ears of corn)
- 1 red bell pepper, diced
- 1 cup lima beans (if frozen, thawed; if fresh, shelled)
- 1 medium red onion, finely chopped
- 2 cloves garlic, minced
- 1/4 cup fresh basil leaves, chopped
- 2 tablespoons olive oil
- Salt and pepper, to taste
- 1/2 cup cherry tomatoes, halved
- 1 tablespoon lemon juice

Prep Time: 15 min   Cook Time: 3 hours   Serves: 4

DIRECTIONS

In the slow cooker, combine corn, red bell pepper, lima beans, red onion, and garlic. Drizzle with olive oil and season with salt and pepper. Gently stir to combine. Cover and cook on low for about 2-3 hours, or until vegetables are tender. About 30 minutes before serving, stir in the fresh basil, cherry tomatoes, and lemon juice. Allow the flavors to meld together for the remaining cooking time.

NUTRITIONAL INFORMATION

Per serving: 220 calories, 6g protein, 40g carbohydrates, 7g fat, 6g fiber, 0mg cholesterol, 15mg sodium, 500mg potassium

Toasted Sesame & Ginger Bok Choy

INGREDIENTS

- 6 medium heads of bok choy, cleaned and cut into halves
- 3 tablespoons toasted sesame oil
- 2 tablespoons soy sauce (or tamari for gluten-free)
- 1 tablespoon fresh ginger, grated
- 3 garlic cloves, minced
- 2 tablespoons toasted sesame seeds
- 2 green onions, sliced for garnish

Prep Time: 10 min   Cook Time: 2 hours   Serves: 4

DIRECTIONS

In a mixing bowl, whisk together sesame oil, soy sauce, grated ginger, and minced garlic. Place the bok choy halves into the slow cooker and pour the sauce mixture over them, ensuring each piece is coated. Cover and cook on low for about 2 hours or until the bok choy is tender but not mushy. Prior to serving, sprinkle with toasted sesame seeds and sliced green onions.

NUTRITIONAL INFORMATION

Per serving: 90 calories, 3g protein, 7g carbohydrates, 6g fat, 2g fiber, 0mg cholesterol, 540mg sodium, 400mg potassium.

Slow-Cooked Ratatouille Medley

INGREDIENTS

- 1 large eggplant, diced
- 1 zucchini, sliced
- 1 yellow squash, sliced
- 1 red bell pepper, chopped
- 1 green bell pepper, chopped
- 1 medium onion, diced
- 3 garlic cloves, minced
- 1 can (28 oz.) of diced tomatoes, drained
- 1/4 cup fresh basil, chopped
- 2 teaspoons dried oregano
- 1 teaspoon salt (adjust to preference)
- 1/2 teaspoon black pepper
- 2 tablespoons olive oil
- 1 tablespoon balsamic vinegar

 Prep Time: 20 min

 Cook Time: 4 hours

 Serves: 4

DIRECTIONS

In the slow cooker, combine eggplant, zucchini, squash, bell peppers, onion, garlic, and diced tomatoes. In a separate bowl, mix together basil, oregano, salt, pepper, olive oil, and balsamic vinegar. Pour this mixture over the vegetables in the slow cooker and gently stir to combine. Cover and cook on low for 4 hours, or until all vegetables are tender. Before serving, adjust seasoning if necessary and garnish with additional fresh basil.

NUTRITIONAL INFORMATION

Per serving: 150 calories, 4g protein, 26g carbohydrates, 5g fat, 8g fiber, 0mg cholesterol, 650mg sodium, 800mg potassium.

Zesty Citrus Asparagus Spears

INGREDIENTS

- 1 pound fresh asparagus, trimmed
- Zest and juice of 1 lemon
- Zest and juice of 1 orange
- 2 tablespoons olive oil
- 3 garlic cloves, minced
- 1/4 teaspoon red pepper flakes (adjust to preference)
- Salt and black pepper, to taste
- 2 tablespoons fresh parsley, chopped (for garnish)

 Prep Time: 10 min

 Cook Time: 2 hours

 Serves: 4

DIRECTIONS

In a small bowl, mix together lemon zest, lemon juice, orange zest, orange juice, olive oil, minced garlic, red pepper flakes, salt, and black pepper. Place the asparagus spears in the slow cooker and pour the citrus mixture over them, ensuring all spears are coated. Cover and cook on low for 2 hours or until asparagus is tender but still slightly crisp. Before serving, garnish with fresh parsley.

NUTRITIONAL INFORMATION

Per serving: 90 calories, 3g protein, 10g carbohydrates, 5g fat, 3g fiber, 0mg cholesterol, 10mg sodium, 300mg potassium.

Caramelized Onion & Mushroom Compote

INGREDIENTS

- 4 large onions, thinly sliced
- 16 oz (450g) mixed mushrooms (such as button, shiitake, and cremini), sliced
- 3 tablespoons olive oil
- 4 garlic cloves, minced
- 2 tablespoons balsamic vinegar
- 1 tablespoon fresh thyme leaves (or 1 teaspoon dried thyme)
- Salt and black pepper, to taste
- 1/4 cup vegetable broth or water

Prep Time: 15 min   Cook Time: 6 hours   Serves: 4 servings

DIRECTIONS

In the slow cooker, combine onions, mushrooms, olive oil, garlic, balsamic vinegar, thyme, salt, and pepper. Mix well to ensure all ingredients are coated in the olive oil and vinegar. Pour the vegetable broth or water over the mixture.

Cover and cook on low for 6 hours, stirring occasionally, until onions are deeply caramelized and mushrooms are tender. Before serving, adjust seasoning if needed.

NUTRITIONAL INFORMATION

Per serving: 180 calories, 4g protein, 24g carbohydrates, 9g fat, 4g fiber, 0mg cholesterol, 150mg sodium, 450mg potassium.

Herb-Infused Polenta Cakes

INGREDIENTS

- 1 cup coarse cornmeal (polenta)
- 4 cups vegetable broth or water
- 2 tablespoons olive oil
- 2 cloves garlic, minced
- 1/4 cup mixed fresh herbs (like rosemary, thyme, and parsley), finely chopped
- 1 teaspoon sea salt
- 1/2 teaspoon freshly ground black pepper
- 1/4 cup nutritional yeast (optional for a cheesy flavor)

Prep Time: 10 min   Cook Time: 4 hours   Serves: 4

DIRECTIONS

In the slow cooker, whisk together the cornmeal, vegetable broth, olive oil, and garlic until well combined and there are no lumps. Cover and cook on high for 4 hours, stirring occasionally to prevent sticking or clumping. About 30 minutes before the cooking time is done, stir in the finely chopped herbs, salt, pepper, and nutritional yeast (if using). After cooking, transfer the thickened polenta to a parchment-lined baking dish, smooth the top, and refrigerate for at least 2 hours. Once set, cut into desired cake shapes. For serving, you can sear the polenta cakes in a hot skillet for a crispy exterior or enjoy as is.

NUTRITIONAL INFORMATION

Per serving: 210 calories, 5g protein, 35g carbohydrates, 6g fat, 4g fiber, 0mg cholesterol, 600mg sodium, 120mg potassium.

Buttery Vegan Mashed Potatoes

INGREDIENTS

- 2 lbs russet potatoes, peeled and cut into 2-inch chunks
- 3 cups vegetable broth
- 4 cloves garlic, minced
- 1/2 cup vegan butter (e.g., Earth Balance)
- 1/2 cup unsweetened almond milk or any plant-based milk
- Salt and pepper, to taste
- Fresh chives or parsley for garnish (optional)

Prep Time: 15 min

Cook Time: 4 hours

Serves: 4

DIRECTIONS

Place the potato chunks, garlic, and vegetable broth in the slow cooker. Ensure the potatoes are submerged; add water if necessary. Cover and cook on high for 4 hours or until the potatoes are fork-tender. Drain the potatoes and return them to the slow cooker. Add the vegan butter, almond milk, salt, and pepper.

Mash until smooth and creamy, adjusting consistency with more milk or butter as needed. Taste and adjust seasoning if necessary. Serve hot, garnished with chives or parsley if desired.

NUTRITIONAL INFORMATION

Per serving: 320 calories, 4g protein, 50g carbohydrates, 12g fat, 5g fiber, 0mg cholesterol, 650mg sodium, 900mg potassium.

Red Cabbage & Apple Slaw

INGREDIENTS

- 1/2 medium-sized red cabbage, thinly sliced
- 2 apples, cored and thinly sliced (preferably a crisp variety like Fuji or Honeycrisp)
- 1/4 cup apple cider vinegar
- 2 tablespoons maple syrup or agave nectar
- 1 tablespoon olive oil
- 1/2 teaspoon salt
- 1/4 teaspoon black pepper
- 2 tablespoons fresh parsley, finely chopped
- 2 tablespoons chia seeds (optional for added nutrition)

Prep Time: 15 min

Cook Time: 2 hours

Serves: 4 servings

DIRECTIONS

In the slow cooker, combine red cabbage, apples, apple cider vinegar, maple syrup, olive oil, salt, and pepper. Gently toss to mix. Cover and cook on low for 2 hours. The slaw should be slightly softened but still have a crunch. Before serving, mix in the fresh parsley and chia seeds, if using. Adjust seasoning if necessary. Serve either warm or allow it to cool for a refreshing side dish.

NUTRITIONAL INFORMATION

Per serving: 150 calories, 3g protein, 30g carbohydrates, 4g fat, 6g fiber, 0mg cholesterol, 300mg sodium, 400mg potassium.

Lemon & Garlic Sautéed Spinach

INGREDIENTS

- 16 oz fresh spinach, washed and roughly chopped
- 3 garlic cloves, minced
- Zest and juice of 1 lemon
- 2 tablespoons olive oil
- 1/2 teaspoon salt
- 1/4 teaspoon freshly ground black pepper

Prep Time: 10 min

Cook Time: 1.5 hours

Serves: 4 servings

DIRECTIONS

In the slow cooker, combine spinach, minced garlic, lemon zest, lemon juice, olive oil, salt, and pepper. Toss gently to coat the spinach. Cover and cook on low for 1.5 hours. The spinach should be wilted but still vibrant in color. Before serving, give the spinach a good stir to mix in the flavors and ensure everything is warmed through. Adjust seasoning if necessary and serve immediately.

NUTRITIONAL INFORMATION

Per serving: 80 calories, 3g protein, 6g carbohydrates, 6g fat, 2g fiber, 0mg cholesterol, 350mg sodium, 500mg potassium.

Sauces, Dips, & Spreads

Creamy Vegan Tzatziki Sauce

INGREDIENTS

- 1 cup unsweetened coconut yogurt (or any other plant-based yogurt)
- 1 cucumber, peeled, deseeded, and finely grated
- 3 cloves garlic, minced
- 2 tablespoons fresh dill, finely chopped
- Juice of 1 lemon
- 2 tablespoons olive oil
- Salt to taste
- Freshly ground black pepper to taste

 Prep Time: 10 min

 Cook Time: 2 hours

 Serves: 4

DIRECTIONS

Start by squeezing out as much liquid as possible from the grated cucumber. You can do this by placing the grated cucumber in a sieve and pressing it with the back of a spoon or using a cheesecloth. In the slow cooker, combine the coconut yogurt, squeezed cucumber, minced garlic, dill, lemon juice, olive oil, salt, and pepper. Cover and cook on the lowest setting for 2 hours to let the flavors meld. Stir well before serving. Adjust seasoning if necessary and serve chilled.

NUTRITIONAL INFORMATION

Per serving: 120 calories, 2g protein, 6g carbohydrates, 10g fat, 1g fiber, 0mg cholesterol, 80mg sodium, 150mg potassium.

Sun-Dried Tomato & Basil Pesto

INGREDIENTS

- 1 cup sun-dried tomatoes (not in oil), soaked in warm water for 30 minutes and drained
- 1 cup fresh basil leaves, tightly packed
- 3 cloves garlic, peeled
- 1/4 cup pine nuts or walnuts
- 1/4 cup nutritional yeast (as a vegan Parmesan substitute)
- 1/4 cup extra-virgin olive oil
- Salt and black pepper, to taste
- 1/4 cup water (or more as needed to adjust consistency)

 Prep Time: 10 min

 Cook Time: 1 hour

 Serves: 4 servings

DIRECTIONS

Start by placing the soaked and drained sun-dried tomatoes, basil, garlic, nuts, nutritional yeast, olive oil, salt, and black pepper in a blender or food processor. Pulse until the mixture is finely chopped. Transfer the mixture to the slow cooker and add water. Mix to combine. Cover and cook on low for 1 hour, allowing the flavors to meld together. Check the consistency. If you prefer a looser pesto, add a bit more water and stir.

NUTRITIONAL INFORMATION

Per serving: 210 calories, 6g protein, 12g carbohydrates, 16g fat, 4g fiber, 0mg cholesterol, 120mg sodium, 350mg potassium.

Spicy Chipotle Black Bean Dip

INGREDIENTS

- 2 cups cooked black beans (or one 15 oz. can, drained and rinsed)
- 1-2 chipotle peppers in adobo sauce, finely chopped (adjust to taste)
- 3 cloves garlic, minced
- 1/4 cup chopped fresh cilantro
- Juice of 1 lime
- 1/2 teaspoon ground cumin
- 1/4 cup water or vegetable broth
- 1 tablespoon extra-virgin olive oil (optional, for a richer flavor)

 Prep Time: 15 min

 Cook Time: 2 hours

 Serves: 4

DIRECTIONS

In a blender or food processor, blend black beans, chipotle peppers, garlic, cilantro, lime juice, cumin, salt, and water (or broth) until mostly smooth. If you prefer a chunkier texture, pulse fewer times. Transfer the mixture to the slow cooker and stir in the olive oil if using. Cover and cook on low for 2 hours. Once done, garnish with diced red onion before serving.

NUTRITIONAL INFORMATION

Per serving: 170 calories, 9g protein, 27g carbohydrates, 3g fat, 8g fiber, 0mg cholesterol, 250mg sodium, 600mg potassium.

Slow-Cooked Marinara Bliss

INGREDIENTS

- 1 can (28 oz.) crushed tomatoes
- 5 fresh Roma tomatoes, diced
- 1 large onion, finely chopped
- 4 cloves garlic, minced
- 2 tablespoons olive oil
- 1/4 cup fresh basil
- 1/4 cup fresh parsley
- 1 teaspoon dried oregano
- 1/2 teaspoon red pepper flakes (optional, for a touch of heat)
- 1 teaspoon sugar
- 1/4 cup water or vegetable broth

 Prep Time: 15 min

 Cook Time: 6 hours

 Serves: 4 servings

DIRECTIONS

In your slow cooker, combine crushed tomatoes, Roma tomatoes, onion, garlic, olive oil, herbs, red pepper flakes, sugar, salt, and black pepper. Pour in the water or vegetable broth to achieve desired consistency. Stir until everything is well mixed. Cover and cook on low for 6 hours, stirring occasionally if possible. Before serving, adjust seasoning if necessary and stir in the fresh basil and parsley for that burst of freshness.

NUTRITIONAL INFORMATION

Per serving: 140 calories, 3g protein, 19g carbohydrates, 7g fat, 4g fiber, 0mg cholesterol, 300mg sodium, 600mg potassium.

Cashew & Garlic Alfredo Sauce

INGREDIENTS

- 1 cup raw cashews, soaked for at least 4 hours or overnight
- 2 1/2 cups water or unsweetened almond milk
- 5 cloves garlic, minced
- 1 tablespoon olive oil
- 1/4 cup nutritional yeast (for a cheesy flavor)
- 1 teaspoon onion powder
- Salt and white pepper to taste
- Juice of half a lemon
- Optional: 1 tablespoon of fresh chopped parsley for garnish

Prep Time: 10 min   Cook Time: 2 hours   Serves: 4

DIRECTIONS

After soaking, drain and rinse the cashews thoroughly. In the slow cooker, combine cashews, water or almond milk, minced garlic, olive oil, nutritional yeast, onion powder, salt, and white pepper. Cover and cook on low for 2 hours, stirring occasionally. Once cooked, blend the mixture using a blender or immersion blender until smooth and creamy. Add lemon juice and adjust seasoning as needed. Serve over your favorite plant-based pasta and garnish with fresh parsley, if desired.

NUTRITIONAL INFORMATION

Per serving: 190 calories, 7g protein, 12g carbohydrates, 14g fat, 2g fiber, 0mg cholesterol, 80mg sodium, 320mg potassium.

Smoky Eggplant Baba Ganoush

INGREDIENTS

- 2 medium eggplants
- 3 cloves garlic, minced
- 3 tablespoons tahini (sesame paste)
- Juice of 1 lemon
- 1 teaspoon smoked paprika
- 2 tablespoons olive oil, plus extra for drizzling
- 2 tablespoons chopped fresh parsley
- Salt to taste
- Optional: a pinch of cumin for an extra depth of flavor

 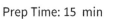

Prep Time: 15 min   Cook Time: 4 hours   Serves: 4

DIRECTIONS

Pierce the eggplants several times with a fork to prevent them from bursting. Place them in the slow cooker. Cover and cook on low for 4 hours, or until the eggplants are tender and collapsing. Once cooked, allow the eggplants to cool slightly. Then, cut them open and scoop out the soft flesh into a bowl. Discard the skin. To the bowl, add minced garlic, tahini, lemon juice, smoked paprika, olive oil, and salt. Blend with a fork or use an immersion blender until mostly smooth with some texture remaining. Adjust seasoning to taste. Transfer to a serving bowl, drizzle with a bit more olive oil, and sprinkle with chopped parsley. Serve with pita bread or vegetable sticks.

NUTRITIONAL INFORMATION

Per serving: 140 calories, 3g protein, 15g carbohydrates, 9g fat, 6g fiber, 0mg cholesterol, 60mg sodium, 390mg potassium.

Pineapple & Jalapeno Salsa

INGREDIENTS

- 2 cups fresh pineapple, diced
- 2 jalapenos, seeded and finely chopped
- 1 red onion, finely diced
- 1/4 cup fresh cilantro, chopped
- Juice of 1 lime
- 1/2 teaspoon salt
- 1/4 teaspoon black pepper

Prep Time: 15 min

Cook Time: 2 hours

Serves: 4

DIRECTIONS

In the slow cooker, combine the diced pineapple, chopped jalapenos, and diced red onion. Cover and set to low heat. Allow the ingredients to meld together for about 2 hours. This will soften the onions and jalapenos slightly and intensify the flavors. After 2 hours, transfer the mixture to a bowl. Stir in the chopped cilantro, lime juice, salt, and black pepper. Adjust seasonings if needed. Serve chilled with tortilla chips or as a topping for grilled dishes.

NUTRITIONAL INFORMATION

Per serving: 60 calories, 1g protein, 15g carbohydrates, 0g fat, 2g fiber, 0mg cholesterol, 290mg sodium, 180mg potassium.

Creamy Avocado & Lime Dip

INGREDIENTS

- 3 ripe avocados, peeled and pitted
- Juice of 2 limes
- 1/4 cup fresh cilantro, chopped
- 2 cloves garlic, minced
- 1/2 teaspoon salt
- 1/4 teaspoon black pepper
- 1/4 cup coconut milk (full fat for creaminess)

Prep Time: 10 min

Cook Time: 1 hou

Serves: 4 servings

DIRECTIONS

In a blender or food processor, combine avocados, lime juice, cilantro, garlic, salt, and pepper. Blend until smooth. Transfer the blended mixture to the slow cooker and stir in the coconut milk to achieve a creamy texture. Cover and set the slow cooker to the "Warm" setting. Allow the dip to meld and warm for about 1 hour. Before serving, give it a good stir and adjust seasonings if needed. Serve warm with tortilla chips or vegetable sticks.

NUTRITIONAL INFORMATION

Per serving: 250 calories, 3g protein, 12g carbohydrates, 23g fat, 7g fiber, 0mg cholesterol, 310mg sodium, 690mg potassium.

Vegan Nacho Cheese Delight

INGREDIENTS

- 1 cup raw cashews (soaked for at least 4 hours and drained)
- 1/4 cup nutritional yeast
- 1 roasted red bell pepper (skin removed)
- 1/2 teaspoon garlic powder
- 1/2 teaspoon onion powder
- 1/2 teaspoon turmeric
- 1/2 teaspoon smoked paprika
- 1/4 teaspoon cayenne pepper (adjust for desired heat)
- 1 teaspoon salt
- 1 cup unsweetened almond milk

Prep Time: 15 min

Cook Time: 2 hours

Serves: 4

DIRECTIONS

In a high-speed blender, combine the soaked cashews, nutritional yeast, roasted bell pepper, garlic powder, onion powder, turmeric, smoked paprika, cayenne pepper, salt, and almond milk. Blend until silky smooth. Transfer the blended mixture to the slow cooker. Cover and set the slow cooker to low. Allow the mixture to heat and meld for about 2 hours, stirring occasionally to ensure even heating. Once heated through and slightly thickened, the nacho cheese is ready to be served. Serve with tortilla chips, drizzled over nachos, or as a dip for veggies.

NUTRITIONAL INFORMATION

Per serving: 220 calories, 8g protein, 15g carbohydrates, 15g fat, 3g fiber, 0mg cholesterol, 600mg sodium, 410mg potassium.

Slow-Roasted Red Pepper Hummus

INGREDIENTS

- 2 cans (15 oz each) chickpeas, rinsed and drained
- 2 roasted red peppers
- 3 cloves garlic, minced
- 3 tablespoons tahini
- Juice of 1 lemon
- 1/4 cup olive oil
- 1/2 teaspoon ground cumin
- Salt to taste
- 1/4 cup water or reserved chickpea liquid for desired consistency

Prep Time: 15 minutes

Cook Time: 2 hours

Serves: 4

DIRECTIONS

In a food processor, blend chickpeas, roasted red peppers, garlic, tahini, lemon juice, olive oil, cumin, and salt until smooth. Transfer the blended hummus mixture to the slow cooker. Set the slow cooker to warm and let the hummus flavors meld and warm slightly for about 2 hours. Stir occasionally. Adjust consistency with water or reserved chickpea liquid if desired. Once done, transfer to a serving bowl and drizzle with a little olive oil, if desired.

NUTRITIONAL INFORMATION

Per serving: 280 calories, 10g protein, 34g carbohydrates, 13g fat, 9g fiber, 0mg cholesterol, 400mg sodium, 350mg potassium.

Sweet & Tangy Barbecue Sauce

INGREDIENTS

- 1 can (15 oz) tomato sauce
- 1/2 cup apple cider vinegar
- 1/4 cup maple syrup or agave nectar
- 2 tablespoons molasses
- 1 tablespoon smoked paprika
- 1 teaspoon garlic powder
- 1 teaspoon onion powder
- 1/2 teaspoon black pepper
- 1/4 teaspoon cayenne pepper (adjust for heat preference)
- 1/2 teaspoon salt

 Prep Time: 10 min

 Cook Time: 4 hours

 Serves: 6

DIRECTIONS

In a mixing bowl, combine all the ingredients and whisk until they are well incorporated. Pour the mixture into the slow cooker. Set the slow cooker on low heat and let the sauce simmer for 4 hours, allowing flavors to meld and sauce to thicken slightly. Stir occasionally. Once done, allow to cool before transferring to an airtight container for storage. Store in the refrigerator.

NUTRITIONAL INFORMATION

Per serving: 70 calories, 1g protein, 17g carbohydrates, 0.2g fat, 1g fiber, 0mg cholesterol, 350mg sodium, 300mg potassium.

Thai Peanut Dipping Sauce

INGREDIENTS

- 1 cup creamy peanut butter (natural, unsweetened)
- 1 can (13.5 oz) coconut milk
- 3 tablespoons soy sauce or tamari
- 2 tablespoons lime juice
- 2 tablespoons agave nectar or maple syrup
- 2 cloves garlic, minced
- 1 tablespoon freshly grated ginger
- 1/2 teaspoon crushed red pepper flakes (adjust for heat preference)

 Prep Time: 10 min

 Cook Time: 2 hours

 Serves: 6

DIRECTIONS

In the slow cooker, combine all ingredients. Set the slow cooker on low heat and cook for 2 hours, stirring occasionally to ensure a smooth consistency. Once done, adjust seasoning if necessary, then transfer to serving bowls. The sauce will thicken as it cools. Serve with fresh spring rolls, grilled veggies, or tofu skewers.

NUTRITIONAL INFORMATION

Per serving: 250 calories, 8g protein, 15g carbohydrates, 19g fat, 3g fiber, 0mg cholesterol, 500mg sodium, 300mg potassium.

Garlic & Herb Vegan Aioli

INGREDIENTS

- 1 cup raw cashews, soaked for at least 4 hours and drained
- 5-6 garlic cloves
- 1 tablespoon olive oil
- 2 teaspoons lemon juice
- 1/2 cup unsweetened almond milk (or another plant-based milk of your choice)
- 1 tablespoon fresh chopped parsley
- 1 tablespoon fresh chopped chives
- 1/2 teaspoon sea salt (or to taste)
- 1/4 teaspoon black pepper

 Prep Time: 10 min

 Cook Time: 1 hour

 Serves: 4

DIRECTIONS

In a small pan over low heat, add the olive oil and garlic cloves. Cook gently until the garlic is soft and lightly golden. This will take about 10 minutes. Remove from heat and allow to cool. In the slow cooker, combine the soaked cashews, soft garlic cloves, lemon juice, almond milk, salt, and pepper. Cover and cook on low for 1 hour. After cooking, let the mixture cool slightly. Transfer the mixture to a blender or food processor. Blend until smooth. Stir in the chopped parsley and chives. Transfer to a container and refrigerate until chilled. The aioli will thicken as it cools.

NUTRITIONAL INFORMATION

Per serving: 200 calories, 5g protein, 10g carbohydrates, 16g fat, 1g fiber, 0mg cholesterol, 320mg sodium, 250mg potassium.

Caramelized Onion & Olive Tapenade

INGREDIENTS

- 3 large onions, thinly sliced
- 2 tablespoons olive oil
- 1 cup mixed olives (green and black), pitted and roughly chopped
- 3 garlic cloves, minced
- 2 tablespoons capers, drained and rinsed
- 1 tablespoon balsamic vinegar
- Zest and juice of 1 lemon
- 1/4 teaspoon freshly ground black pepper
- 2 tablespoons fresh parsley, finely chopped

 Prep Time: 15 min

 Cook Time: 3 hours

 Serves: 4

DIRECTIONS

In the slow cooker, combine the onions with olive oil, ensuring that the onions are well-coated. Cook on low for 2.5 hours, or until the onions are soft and caramelized. Add the chopped olives, garlic, capers, balsamic vinegar, lemon zest, lemon juice, and black pepper to the slow cooker. Mix well and continue to cook for an additional 30 minutes. Turn off the slow cooker and let the mixture cool slightly. If you prefer a smoother texture, you can pulse the tapenade a few times in a food processor. Stir in the fresh parsley and transfer to a serving bowl. Serve chilled or at room temperature.

NUTRITIONAL INFORMATION

Per serving: 190 calories, 2g protein, 12g carbohydrates, 15g fat, 3g fiber, 0mg cholesterol, 500mg sodium, 250mg potassium.

Tangy Vegan Tofu Ricotta Spread

INGREDIENTS

- 14 oz firm tofu, drained and crumbled
- 1/4 cup nutritional yeast
- 3 garlic cloves, minced
- 2 tablespoons olive oil
- 2 tablespoons lemon juice
- 1 tablespoon apple cider vinegar
- 1 teaspoon dried basil
- 1 teaspoon dried oregano
- Salt and pepper to taste
- 2 tablespoons fresh parsley, finely chopped (optional)

Prep Time: 10 min

Cook Time: 1 hour

Serves: 4

DIRECTIONS

In a bowl, mix crumbled tofu, nutritional yeast, garlic, olive oil, lemon juice, apple cider vinegar, basil, and oregano until well combined. Transfer the mixture to the slow cooker, spreading it out evenly. Cook on low for 1 hour, occasionally stirring to prevent sticking and to ensure even cooking. After cooking, season with salt and pepper to taste. Stir in fresh parsley if using. Allow to cool slightly before transferring to a container. Store in the refrigerator and serve chilled or at room temperature.

NUTRITIONAL INFORMATION

Per serving: 150 calories, 11g protein, 6g carbohydrates, 9g fat, 3g fiber, 0mg cholesterol, 150mg sodium, 250mg potassium.

Global Inspirations

Indian Vegetable & Lentil Korma

INGREDIENTS

- 1 cup dry lentils (green or brown), rinsed and drained
- 2 cups mixed vegetables, chopped
- 1 large onion, finely chopped
- 3 garlic cloves, minced
- 1-inch ginger, grated
- 2 cups coconut milk
- 2 tablespoons tomato paste, almond or cashew butter
- 2 teaspoons garam masala
- 1 teaspoon ground turmeric, cumin

Prep Time: 20 min

Cook Time: 6 hours

Serves: 4

DIRECTIONS

In the slow cooker, combine lentils, mixed vegetables, onion, garlic, and ginger.

In a separate bowl, whisk together coconut milk, tomato paste, almond or cashew butter, and all the spices until smooth. Pour this mixture over the vegetables and lentils in the slow cooker. Stir well to ensure everything is combined and coated with the sauce. Cook on low for 6 hours, or until the lentils and vegetables are tender. Adjust seasonings if necessary, garnish with fresh cilantro before serving.

NUTRITIONAL INFORMATION

Per serving: 380 calories, 16g protein, 45g carbohydrates, 18g fat, 15g fiber, 0mg cholesterol, 220mg sodium, 850mg potassium.

Thai Green Curry with Tofu

INGREDIENTS

- 14 oz (400g) firm tofu, pressed and cubed
- 2 cans (800 ml) of full-fat coconut milk
- 3 tablespoons green curry paste
- 2 medium zucchinis, sliced
- 1 red bell pepper
- 1 cup snap peas, trimmed
- 1 large onion
- 3 garlic cloves, minced
- 1 tablespoon freshly grated ginger
- 2 tablespoons soy sauce or tamari
- 1 tablespoon coconut sugar or brown sugar

Prep Time: 25 min

Cook Time: 4 hours

Serves: 4

DIRECTIONS

In the slow cooker, add coconut milk, green curry paste, soy sauce, coconut sugar, garlic, and ginger. Stir well to combine. Add the tofu, zucchinis, red bell pepper, snap peas, and onion into the slow cooker and gently stir to coat the ingredients with the curry mixture. Cook on low for 4 hours, ensuring the vegetables are tender but not overly soft. Before serving, stir in lime juice and adjust seasoning with salt if necessary. Garnish with fresh basil.

NUTRITIONAL INFORMATION

Per serving: 440 calories, 16g protein, 35g carbohydrates, 29g fat, 5g fiber, 0mg cholesterol, 480mg sodium, 680mg potassium.

Mexican Vegan Pozole Rojo

INGREDIENTS

- 2 cans (30 oz) hominy, drained and rinsed
- 2 ancho chilies, stems and seeds removed
- 2 guajillo chilies, stems and seeds removed
- 4 cups vegetable broth
- 1 medium onion, chopped
- 4 garlic cloves, minced
- 1 can (15 oz) diced tomatoes
- 1 zucchini, cubed
- 1 red bell pepper, diced
- 2 teaspoons dried oregano
- 1 teaspoon ground cumin

 Prep Time: 20 min

 Cook Time: 6 hours

 Serves: 4

DIRECTIONS

Place the ancho and guajillo chilies in a bowl and cover with hot water. Let them soak for about 15 minutes, then blend with a little bit of the soaking water until smooth. In the slow cooker, combine the chili paste, hominy, vegetable broth, onion, garlic, diced tomatoes, zucchini, red bell pepper, oregano, and cumin. Stir to mix everything together. Cook on low for 6 hours. Season with salt and pepper to taste. Serve in bowls and garnish with avocado, cilantro, lime, and radish slices.

NUTRITIONAL INFORMATION

Per serving: 280 calories, 9g protein, 60g carbohydrates, 3g fat, 11g fiber, 0mg cholesterol, 650mg sodium, 470mg potassium.

Japanese Miso & Vegetable Stew

INGREDIENTS

- 4 cups vegetable broth
- 3 tablespoons white miso paste
- 1 medium-sized daikon radish, peeled and sliced into half-moons
- 2 medium-sized carrots, sliced into thin rounds
- 1 cup snap peas, trimmed
- 1 cup shiitake mushrooms
- 1/2 cup firm tofu, cubed
- 2 green onions, thinly
- 1 tablespoon soy sauce, mirin
- 1 sheet nori seaweed
- 1 teaspoon grated fresh ginger

 Prep Time: 15 min

 Cook Time: 4 hours

 Serves: 4

DIRECTIONS

In a bowl, whisk together the miso paste with a bit of vegetable broth until smooth. Add this miso mixture, the rest of the vegetable broth, daikon, carrots, snap peas, mushrooms, tofu, green onions, soy sauce, mirin, nori, and ginger to the slow cooker. Stir gently to combine. Cook on low for 4 hours until the vegetables are tender. Before serving, check and adjust the seasoning if needed. Serve in bowls and garnish with cilantro and sesame seeds.

NUTRITIONAL INFORMATION

Per serving: 120 calories, 7g protein, 25g carbohydrates, 1g fat, 5g fiber, 0mg cholesterol, 800mg sodium, 490mg potassium.

Ethiopian Berbere-Spiced Chickpea Stew

INGREDIENTS

- 2 cups dried chickpeas, soaked overnight and drained
- 4 cups vegetable broth
- 1 large onion
- 3 garlic cloves, minced
- 1 tablespoon ginger, minced
- 3 tablespoons tomato paste
- 2 tablespoons berbere spice mix
- 1 can (14 oz.) diced tomatoes
- 2 medium-sized carrots, chopped
- 1 red bell pepper, chopped

 Prep Time: 20 min

 Cook Time: 6 hours

 Serves: 4

DIRECTIONS

In your slow cooker, combine chickpeas, vegetable broth, onion, garlic, ginger, tomato paste, berbere spice, diced tomatoes, carrots, and bell pepper. Drizzle with olive oil and sprinkle in the salt. Stir well to combine all the ingredients. Cover and cook on low for 6 hours or until the chickpeas are tender and flavors melded. Before serving, check and adjust seasoning if needed. Serve hot, garnished with cilantro and accompanied by lemon wedges.

NUTRITIONAL INFORMATION

Per serving: 280 calories, 11g protein, 45g carbohydrates, 7g fat, 12g fiber, 0mg cholesterol, 690mg sodium, 720mg potassium.

Italian Vegan Osso Buco

INGREDIENTS

- 4 large king oyster mushrooms, stems cut into thick slices
- 2 tablespoons olive oil
- 1 large onion, finely chopped
- 2 garlic cloves, minced
- 1 large carrot, diced
- 2 celery stalks, diced
- 1 cup dry white wine (vegan-friendly)
- 2 cups vegetable broth
- 1 can (14 oz.) crushed tomatoes
- 2 bay leaves
- 1 teaspoon dried thyme
- 1 teaspoon dried rosemary

 Prep Time: 25 minutes

 Cook Time: 6 hours

 Serves: 4

DIRECTIONS

Heat olive oil in a skillet over medium heat. Add king oyster mushroom slices and sear until golden brown on both sides. Transfer them to the slow cooker. In the same skillet, sauté onion, garlic, carrot, and celery until soft. Add the wine and let it simmer for a few minutes to evaporate the alcohol. Transfer the sautéed vegetables and wine mixture to the slow cooker. Add vegetable broth, crushed tomatoes, bay leaves, thyme, rosemary, salt, and pepper. Stir well. Cover and cook on low for 6 hours. Before serving, sprinkle with lemon zest and fresh parsley.

NUTRITIONAL INFORMATION

Per serving: 180 calories, 5g protein, 28g carbohydrates, 5g fat, 6g fiber, 0mg cholesterol, 680mg sodium, 720mg potassium.

Middle Eastern Lentil & Spinach Soup

INGREDIENTS

- 1 cup dried green lentils, rinsed and drained
- 4 cups vegetable broth
- 1 large onion, finely chopped
- 3 cloves garlic, minced
- 2 cups fresh spinach, roughly chopped
- 1 can (14 oz.) diced tomatoes
- 2 teaspoons ground cumin
- 1 teaspoon ground coriander
- 1/2 teaspoon ground turmeric
- 1/4 teaspoon cayenne pepper

 Prep Time: 20 min

  Cook Time: 6 hours

 Serves: 4

DIRECTIONS

In a skillet over medium heat, sauté onions and garlic in olive oil until translucent. Transfer sautéed onions and garlic to the slow cooker, and add lentils, vegetable broth, diced tomatoes, cumin, coriander, turmeric, and cayenne pepper. Stir well to combine. Cover and cook on low for 5 hours. After 5 hours, add chopped spinach and lemon juice to the soup. Continue cooking for an additional 1 hour. Season with salt and pepper to taste. Serve hot, garnished with fresh parsley if desired.

NUTRITIONAL INFORMATION

Per serving: 220 calories, 14g protein, 36g carbohydrates, 3g fat, 15g fiber, 0mg cholesterol, 750mg sodium, 740mg potassium.

Spanish Vegetable & Saffron Paella

INGREDIENTS

- 1 1/2 cups Arborio rice or paella rice
- 3 cups vegetable broth
- 1 pinch saffron threads
- 1 large onion, diced
- 3 cloves garlic, minced
- 1 red bell pepper, sliced
- 1 yellow bell pepper, sliced
- 1/2 cup green peas (frozen or fresh)
- 2 medium tomatoes, diced
- 1/2 cup green beans, chopped
- 1/4 cup olive oil
- 1 teaspoon smoked paprika

 Prep Time: 25 min

 Cook Time: 3 hours

 Serves: 4

DIRECTIONS

In a small bowl, warm 1/2 cup of vegetable broth and steep the saffron threads for about 10 minutes. In the slow cooker, heat olive oil on a high setting. Add onions, garlic, red and yellow bell peppers. Sauté for 2-3 minutes until the onions are translucent. Add the rice to the slow cooker, stirring to coat with the oil and veggies. Pour in the saffron-infused broth, the remaining vegetable broth, tomatoes, green beans, peas, smoked paprika, salt, and pepper. Cover and cook on low for 3 hours or until rice is tender and has absorbed the liquid. Serve paella garnished with lemon wedges and a sprinkle of fresh parsley.

NUTRITIONAL INFORMATION

Per serving: 410 calories, 8g protein, 70g carbohydrates, 10g fat, 5g fiber, 0mg cholesterol, 680mg sodium, 420mg potassium.

Korean Gochujang Tofu & Veggie Hotpot

INGREDIENTS

- 14 oz (400g) firm tofu, cubed
- 4 cups vegetable broth
- 2 tablespoons gochujang (Korean red chili paste)
- 1 tablespoon soy sauce
- 2 teaspoons sesame oil
- 3 cloves garlic, minced
- 1 inch ginger, minced
- 1 large zucchini, sliced
- 2 carrots, sliced
- 1 bell pepper, sliced
- 1/2 cup mushrooms, sliced
- 1 onion, thinly sliced
- 2 green onions, chopped

Prep Time: 20 min

Cook Time: 4 hours

Serves: 4

DIRECTIONS

In a bowl, mix gochujang, soy sauce, sesame oil, garlic, and ginger until well combined. In the slow cooker, pour in the vegetable broth followed by the gochujang mixture and stir until combined. Add tofu, zucchini, carrots, bell pepper, mushrooms, onion, and half of the green onions to the slow cooker. Stir gently to ensure all ingredients are coated with the sauce. Cover and cook on low for 4 hours. Check occasionally and add a little water if needed. Serve hot, garnished with remaining green onions, sesame seeds, and nori seaweed pieces.

NUTRITIONAL INFORMATION

Per serving: 220 calories, 15g protein, 28g carbohydrates, 7g fat, 5g fiber, 0mg cholesterol, 700mg sodium, 800mg potassium.

Caribbean Coconut & Vegetable Curry

INGREDIENTS

- 1 can (14 oz) coconut milk
- 2 tablespoons curry powder
- 1 tablespoon ground turmeric
- 1 tablespoon ground cumin
- 1 teaspoon ground allspice
- 1 red bell pepper, sliced
- 1 yellow bell pepper, sliced
- 2 carrots, peeled and sliced
- 1 zucchini, diced
- 1 onion, finely chopped
- 2 cloves garlic, minced
- 1 thumb-sized piece of ginger, minced
- 1 cup diced tomatoes
- 1 habanero pepper

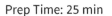

Prep Time: 25 min

Cook Time: 5 hours

Serves: 4

DIRECTIONS

In a bowl, whisk together coconut milk, curry powder, turmeric, cumin, allspice, and salt until smooth. Place the sliced bell peppers, carrots, zucchini, onion, garlic, ginger, diced tomatoes, and habanero pepper (if using) into the slow cooker. Pour the coconut milk mixture over the vegetables in the slow cooker, stirring gently to combine. Cover and cook on low for 5 hours, or until the vegetables are tender. Before serving, stir in the lime juice and adjust seasoning if necessary. Garnish with fresh cilantro.

NUTRITIONAL INFORMATION

Per serving: 280 calories, 6g protein, 25g carbohydrates, 20g fat, 7g fiber, 0mg cholesterol, 80mg sodium, 700mg potassium.

Greek Vegan Moussaka

INGREDIENTS

- 2 large eggplants, thinly sliced
- 3 potatoes, thinly sliced
- 1 can (14 oz) of lentils, drained and rinsed, tomatoes, diced
- 1 onion, finely chopped
- 2 cloves garlic, minced
- 3 tablespoons tomato paste
- 2 teaspoons dried oregano
- 1 teaspoon cinnamon
- 1/4 teaspoon ground cloves
- 2 cups unsweetened almond milk

Prep Time: 30 min   Cook Time: 4 hours   Serves: 4

DIRECTIONS

Lightly oil eggplant and potato slices, layer them in a slow cooker. Mix lentils, onion, garlic, tomatoes, tomato paste, spices; pour over layers. Top with remaining slices. In a saucepan, make a roux with olive oil and flour. Gradually whisk in almond milk until smooth, add nutritional yeast or vegan cheese if desired. Pour over slow cooker ingredients. Cook on low for 4 hours until vegetables are tender.

NUTRITIONAL INFORMATION

Per serving: 450 calories, 15g protein, 70g carbohydrates, 12g fat, 17g fiber, 0mg cholesterol, 340mg sodium, 1100mg potassium.

Moroccan Lentil & Vegetable Tagine

INGREDIENTS

- 1 cup dried green lentils, rinsed and drained
- 2 carrots, chopped
- 1 zucchini, chopped
- 1 bell pepper
- 1 onion, finely chopped
- 3 cloves garlic, minced
- 1 can (14 oz) diced tomatoes
- 3 cups vegetable broth
- 2 teaspoons ground cumin, coriander
- 1 teaspoon ground turmeric
- 1/2 teaspoon cinnamon
- 1/4 teaspoon cayenne pepper
- 1/4 cup raisins or chopped dried apricots

Prep Time: 20 min   Cook Time: 6 hours   Serves: 4

DIRECTIONS

In a skillet over medium heat, sauté the onions and garlic in olive oil until translucent. Transfer the sautéed onions and garlic to the slow cooker. Add lentils, carrots, zucchini, bell pepper, diced tomatoes, vegetable broth, cumin, coriander, turmeric, cinnamon, cayenne, raisins or apricots, salt, and pepper.
Stir well to ensure all ingredients are well combined. Cover and cook on low for 6 hours or until lentils and vegetables are tender. Before serving, adjust seasoning if necessary and garnish with fresh cilantro or parsley.

NUTRITIONAL INFORMATION

Per serving: 360 calories, 18g protein, 65g carbohydrates, 4g fat, 20g fiber, 0mg cholesterol, 480mg sodium, 950mg potassium.

French Ratatouille Rhapsody

INGREDIENTS

- 1 eggplant, diced
- 1 zucchini, sliced
- 1 yellow squash, sliced
- 1 red bell pepper, chopped
- 1 green bell pepper, chopped
- 1 onion, finely chopped
- 3 cloves garlic, minced
- 1 can (14 oz) diced tomatoes
- 3 tablespoons extra virgin olive oil
- 1 teaspoon dried basil
- 1 teaspoon dried thyme

Prep Time: 25 min

Cook Time: 4 hours

Serves: 4

DIRECTIONS

In a skillet over medium heat, sauté the onions and garlic in 2 tablespoons of olive oil until they're translucent. Transfer the sautéed onions and garlic to the slow cooker. Add the diced eggplant, zucchini, yellow squash, bell peppers, diced tomatoes, the remaining olive oil, dried basil, dried thyme, salt, and pepper. Stir everything gently to ensure all ingredients are mixed well. Cover and cook on low for 4 hours or until vegetables are tender. Before serving, adjust seasoning if necessary and garnish with fresh basil.

NUTRITIONAL INFORMATION

Per serving: 210 calories, 4g protein, 28g carbohydrates, 10g fat, 9g fiber, 0mg cholesterol, 330mg sodium, 750mg potassium.

Vietnamese Vegetable Pho

INGREDIENTS

- 8 cups vegetable broth
- 1 large onion, halved and charred
- 3 cloves of garlic, crushed
- 1 thumb-sized piece of ginger, charred and sliced
- 2 cinnamon sticks
- 3 star anise
- 4 cloves
- 2 tablespoons soy sauce or tamari (for gluten-free option)
- 200g rice noodles
- 2 cups of mixed vegetables (broccoli, bell peppers, carrots, mushrooms), sliced thinly

Prep Time: 20 min

Cook Time: 6 hours

Serves: 4

DIRECTIONS

In the slow cooker, combine vegetable broth, charred onion, garlic, ginger, cinnamon sticks, star anise, cloves, and soy sauce. Cover and cook on low for 6 hours. About 30 minutes before serving, remove the onion, ginger, and spices from the broth using a slotted spoon or strainer. Add the sliced vegetables to the slow cooker and let them cook until tender. While the vegetables are cooking, prepare rice noodles according to package instructions. Drain and set aside. To serve, place a portion of rice noodles in each bowl, ladle the broth and vegetables over the noodles, and garnish with fresh herbs, lime wedges, and optional toppings.

NUTRITIONAL INFORMATION

Per serving: 210 calories, 5g protein, 46g carbohydrates, 1g fat, 4g fiber, 0mg cholesterol, 980mg sodium, 430mg potassium.

Peruvian Quinoa & Vegetable Stew

INGREDIENTS

- 1 cup quinoa, rinsed and drained
- 8 cups vegetable broth
- 1 large onion, diced
- 3 cloves garlic, minced
- 1 red bell pepper, diced
- 2 carrots, diced
- 2 potatoes, diced
- 1 cup corn kernels
- 1 can (14 oz) diced tomatoes, undrained
- 1 teaspoon ground cumin
- 1/2 teaspoon smoked paprika
- 2 teaspoons dried oregano
- Salt and pepper to taste
- 1/4 cup chopped fresh cilantro, for garnish
- 1 lime, cut into wedges, for serving

Prep Time: 20 min

Cook Time: 4 hours

Serves: 4

DIRECTIONS

In the slow cooker, combine quinoa, vegetable broth, onion, garlic, bell pepper, carrots, potatoes, corn, diced tomatoes, cumin, smoked paprika, and oregano. Stir to mix the ingredients. Cover and cook on low for 4 hours or until the vegetables are tender and quinoa is cooked through. Before serving, season with salt and pepper according to taste. Ladle the stew into bowls, garnish with chopped cilantro, and serve with a wedge of lime on the side.

NUTRITIONAL INFORMATION

Per serving: 280 calories, 10g protein, 53g carbohydrates, 3g fat, 7g fiber, 0mg cholesterol, 750mg sodium, 580mg potassium.

Desserts & Sweet Treats

Chocolate Lava Pudding Cake

INGREDIENTS

- 1 cup all-purpose flour
- 1/2 cup granulated sugar
- 1/4 cup unsweetened cocoa powder
- 1.5 teaspoons baking powder
- 1/8 teaspoon salt
- 1/2 cup almond milk
- 2 tablespoons coconut oil, melted
- 1 teaspoon pure vanilla extract
- 3/4 cup dark brown sugar, packed
- 1/4 cup unsweetened cocoa powder
- 1 3/4 cups hot water

 Prep Time: 15 min   Cook Time: 2.5 hours    Serves: 4

DIRECTIONS

In a mixing bowl, whisk together flour, granulated sugar, 1/4 cup cocoa powder, baking powder, and salt. Stir in almond milk, melted coconut oil, and vanilla extract until combined. Pour the batter into the slow cooker, spreading it out evenly. In another bowl, combine brown sugar and 1/4 cup cocoa powder. Sprinkle this mixture over the batter in the slow cooker. Gently pour the hot water over everything. Do not stir. Cover and cook on high for 2.5 hours. The center will be molten, but the sides should be set. Turn off the slow cooker and let the pudding cake stand for about 30 minutes before serving.

NUTRITIONAL INFORMATION

Per serving: 420 calories, 5g protein, 88g carbohydrates, 10g fat, 4g fiber, 0mg cholesterol, 250mg sodium, 250mg potassium.

Slow-Cooked Berry Compote

INGREDIENTS

- 2 cups fresh strawberries, hulled and halved
- 1 cup fresh blueberries
- 1 cup fresh raspberries
- 1/4 cup pure maple syrup (or agave nectar)
- Zest and juice of 1 lemon
- 1/2 teaspoon pure vanilla extract
- A pinch of salt

 Prep Time: 10 min   Cook Time: 3 hours   Serves: 4

DIRECTIONS

In the slow cooker, combine strawberries, blueberries, raspberries, maple syrup, lemon zest, lemon juice, vanilla extract, and salt. Cover and cook on low for 3 hours, stirring occasionally, until the berries have softened and released their juices. Once cooked, you can use a potato masher or the back of a spoon to gently mash the berries if you desire a smoother texture. Let the compote cool before transferring to airtight containers. Store in the refrigerator for up to a week.

NUTRITIONAL INFORMATION

Per serving: 120 calories, 1g protein, 30g carbohydrates, 0.5g fat, 4g fiber, 0mg cholesterol, 20mg sodium, 200mg potassium.

Cinnamon & Apple Bread Pudding

INGREDIENTS

- 6 cups day-old sourdough or crusty bread, cubed
- 2 cups almond milk
- 3 medium apples, peeled, cored, and diced
- 1/2 cup pure maple syrup
- 1/4 cup coconut sugar (or brown sugar)
- 2 flax eggs (2 tablespoons ground flaxseed mixed with 6 tablespoons water)
- 1 tablespoon pure vanilla extract, ground cinnamon
- 1/2 teaspoon ground nutmeg

 Prep Time: 20 min

 Cook Time: 2,5 minutes

 Serves: 6

DIRECTIONS

Make flax eggs by mixing ground flaxseed with water; let it sit for 15 minutes. In a large bowl, combine almond milk, maple syrup, coconut sugar, flax eggs, vanilla, cinnamon, nutmeg, and salt. Whisk well. Add bread cubes and diced apples, then pour the mixture into the slow cooker, spreading it evenly. Cover and cook on low for 2 hours 30 minutes until the bread absorbs most liquid and the top forms a slight crust. Serve warm with your preferred vegan ice cream or whipped cream.

NUTRITIONAL INFORMATION

Per serving: 350 calories, 8g protein, 70g carbohydrates, 5g fat, 6g fiber, 0mg cholesterol, 250mg sodium, 300mg potassium.

Coconut & Pineapple Rice Pudding

INGREDIENTS

- 1 cup Arborio rice (or short-grain rice)
- 4 cups coconut milk (full-fat for creamier texture)
- 1/2 cup agave nectar (or maple syrup)
- 1 teaspoon vanilla extract
- 1/4 teaspoon salt
- 1 cup diced fresh pineapple (can also use canned, but ensure it's drained)
- Zest of 1 lime
- Toasted coconut flakes, for garnish (optional)

 Prep Time: 15 minutes

 Cook Time: 2:45 hours

 Serves: 6

DIRECTIONS

In the slow cooker, combine rice, coconut milk, agave nectar, vanilla extract, and salt. Stir well to combine. Cover and cook on low for 2 hours 30 minutes, occasionally stirring to prevent sticking. After 2 hours and 30 minutes, stir in the diced pineapple and lime zest. Cover and continue to cook for an additional 15 minutes. Serve warm in individual bowls, garnished with toasted coconut flakes if desired.

NUTRITIONAL INFORMATION

Per serving: 450 calories, 6g protein, 60g carbohydrates, 22g fat, 2g fiber, 0mg cholesterol, 120mg sodium, 300mg potassium.

Vegan Chocolate Fondue

INGREDIENTS

- 1 cup vegan dark chocolate chips
- 1/2 cup canned coconut milk (full-fat)
- 1/4 cup unsweetened almond milk (or other plant-based milk)
- 2 tablespoons agave nectar (or maple syrup)
- 1 teaspoon pure vanilla extract
- A pinch of sea salt
- Fresh fruits (like strawberries, bananas, and pineapple) for dipping

 Prep Time: 10 min

 Cook Time: 1 hour 30 minutes

 Serves: 4

DIRECTIONS

In the slow cooker, combine the vegan chocolate chips, coconut milk, almond milk, agave nectar, vanilla extract, and a pinch of sea salt. Set the slow cooker to low heat, cover, and allow the mixture to melt, stirring occasionally to ensure smooth consistency. Once melted and smooth, set the slow cooker to the 'warm' setting to keep the fondue liquid and creamy. Serve with fresh fruits or other vegan-friendly dippers of your choice.

NUTRITIONAL INFORMATION

Per serving: 320 calories, 4g protein, 35g carbohydrates, 20g fat, 4g fiber, 0mg cholesterol, 85mg sodium, 290mg potassium.

Peach & Ginger Crumble

INGREDIENTS

- 6 ripe peaches, pitted and sliced
- 1 tablespoon fresh ginger, finely grated
- 1/4 cup maple syrup
- 1 cup old-fashioned rolled oats
- 1/2 cup almond flour
- 1/4 cup coconut oil, melted
- 1/4 cup coconut sugar
- 1/2 teaspoon ground cinnamon
- 1/4 teaspoon salt

 Prep Time: 20 min

 Cook Time: 3 hours

 Serves: 4

DIRECTIONS

In the slow cooker, combine the sliced peaches, grated ginger, and maple syrup, stirring to coat the peaches evenly. In a mixing bowl, combine the rolled oats, almond flour, melted coconut oil, coconut sugar, cinnamon, and salt. Mix until a crumbly mixture forms. Sprinkle the oat mixture evenly over the peaches in the slow cooker. Cover and cook on low for 3 hours, or until the peaches are tender and the topping is golden brown.

NUTRITIONAL INFORMATION

Per serving: 390 calories, 6g protein, 58g carbohydrates, 16g fat, 7g fiber, 0mg cholesterol, 80mg sodium, 450mg potassium.

Banana & Caramel Upside-Down Cake

INGREDIENTS

- 4 ripe bananas, sliced
- 1/2 cup coconut sugar
- 1/4 cup coconut oil, melted
- 1 1/2 cups whole wheat flour
- 2 teaspoons baking powder
- 1/2 teaspoon salt
- 1/2 cup almond milk
- 1 teaspoon vanilla extract
- 1/4 cup maple syrup

 Prep Time: 15 min

 Cook Time: 3 hours

 Serves: 4

DIRECTIONS

In the base of the slow cooker, evenly spread the melted coconut oil, followed by the coconut sugar. This will create the caramel layer. Place the sliced bananas on top of the sugar layer. In a mixing bowl, combine the whole wheat flour, baking powder, and salt. In another bowl, mix together the almond milk, vanilla extract, and maple syrup. Gradually mix the wet ingredients into the dry until just combined. Pour the batter over the bananas in the slow cooker, spreading it evenly. Cover and cook on high for 3 hours, or until a toothpick inserted into the center of the cake comes out clean.

NUTRITIONAL INFORMATION

Per serving: 490 calories, 7g protein, 85g carbohydrates, 15g fat, 6g fiber, 0mg cholesterol, 350mg sodium, 600mg potassium.

Spiced Pumpkin & Walnut Cake

INGREDIENTS

- 1 1/2 cups pumpkin puree (canned or homemade)
- 1/2 cup coconut oil, melted
- 3/4 cup maple syrup or agave nectar
- 2 cups whole wheat flour
- 1 1/2 teaspoons baking powder
- 1/2 teaspoon baking soda
- 2 teaspoons ground cinnamon
- 1/2 teaspoon ground nutmeg
- 1/2 teaspoon ground cloves
- 1/4 teaspoon salt
- 1 cup chopped walnuts

 Prep Time: 20 min

 Cook Time: 3 hours

 Serves: 6

DIRECTIONS

In a large bowl, combine pumpkin puree, melted coconut oil, and maple syrup. Mix until well combined. In another bowl, whisk together whole wheat flour, baking powder, baking soda, cinnamon, nutmeg, cloves, and salt. Gradually add the dry ingredients into the wet mixture, stirring until just combined. Fold in the chopped walnuts. Pour the batter into the slow cooker, ensuring it's spread evenly. Cover and cook on low for 3 hours, or until a toothpick inserted into the center comes out clean.

NUTRITIONAL INFORMATION

Per serving: 530 calories, 9g protein, 68g carbohydrates, 28g fat, 7g fiber, 0mg cholesterol, 280mg sodium, 310mg potassium.

Vanilla & Cherry Clafoutis

INGREDIENTS

- 2 cups fresh cherries, pitted
- 1 cup almond milk (or any other plant-based milk)
- 1/2 cup chickpea flour
- 1/2 cup maple syrup or agave nectar
- 1 teaspoon pure vanilla extract
- 1/4 teaspoon almond extract (optional)
- A pinch of salt
- 1 tablespoon coconut oil (for greasing)
- Icing sugar for dusting (optional)

Prep Time: 15 min

Cook Time: 2.5 hours

Serves: 4

DIRECTIONS

Lightly grease the bottom of the slow cooker with coconut oil. Place the pitted cherries evenly at the bottom. In a mixing bowl, whisk together almond milk, chickpea flour, maple syrup, vanilla extract, almond extract (if using), and a pinch of salt until smooth. Pour the batter over the cherries in the slow cooker. Cover and cook on high for 2.5 hours or until the clafoutis is set but still slightly wobbly in the middle.

NUTRITIONAL INFORMATION

Per serving: 250 calories, 5g protein, 45g carbohydrates, 5g fat, 3g fiber, 0mg cholesterol, 90mg sodium, 300mg potassium.

Berry & Almond Cobbler

INGREDIENTS

- 3 cups mixed berries (like blueberries, raspberries, strawberries, blackberries)
- 1 cup almond flour
- 1/2 cup rolled oats
- 1/4 cup maple syrup or agave nectar
- 1/4 cup almond milk (or any other plant-based milk)
- 2 teaspoons pure vanilla extract
- 1/4 cup slivered almonds
- 1 teaspoon baking powder
- A pinch of salt
- 1 tablespoon coconut oil (for greasing)

Prep Time: 20 min

Cook Time: 3 hours

Serves: 4

DIRECTIONS

Lightly grease the bottom of the slow cooker with coconut oil. Spread the mixed berries evenly at the bottom of the slow cooker. In a mixing bowl, combine almond flour, rolled oats, maple syrup, almond milk, vanilla extract, baking powder, and a pinch of salt. Mix until a batter forms. Drop spoonfuls of the batter over the berries in the slow cooker, then sprinkle the slivered almonds on top. Cover and cook on high for 3 hours or until the cobbler topping has set and turned slightly golden.

NUTRITIONAL INFORMATION

Per serving: 320 calories, 7g protein, 40g carbohydrates, 16g fat, 6g fiber, 0mg cholesterol, 70mg sodium, 230mg potassium.

Chocolate & Peanut Butter Brownie Delight

INGREDIENTS

- 1 cup all-purpose flour or gluten-free flour
- 1/2 cup unsweetened cocoa powder
- 3/4 cup coconut sugar or brown sugar
- 1/2 teaspoon baking powder
- 1/2 cup almond milk or other plant-based milk
- 1/4 cup coconut oil, melted
- 1 teaspoon pure vanilla extract
- 1/2 cup vegan chocolate chips, natural peanut butter, melted
- 1/4 cup hot water

Prep Time: 15 min   Cook Time: 2.5 hours   Serves: 4

DIRECTIONS

In a mixing bowl, whisk together flour, cocoa powder, sugar, baking powder, and salt. Stir in almond milk, melted coconut oil, and vanilla extract until well combined. Fold in the chocolate chips. Spread this brownie batter evenly in the greased slow cooker. Drizzle melted peanut butter over the top of the brownie batter. Using a knife, create swirl patterns. Pour hot water over the mixture, but do not stir. Cover and cook on low for 2.5 hours. The center will be gooey, and the sides will pull away slightly when done.

NUTRITIONAL INFORMATION

Per serving: 550 calories, 12g protein, 75g carbohydrates, 28g fat, 7g fiber, 0mg cholesterol, 150mg sodium, 420mg potassium.

Lemon & Blueberry Slow-Cooked Cake

INGREDIENTS

- 1 1/2 cups all-purpose flour or gluten-free flour
- 3/4 cup coconut sugar or granulated sugar
- 1 1/2 teaspoons baking powder
- A pinch of salt
- Zest and juice of 2 lemons
- 1/2 cup almond milk or other plant-based milk
- 1/3 cup coconut oil, melted
- 1 teaspoon pure vanilla extract
- 1 cup fresh blueberries

Prep Time: 20 minutes   Cook Time: 3 hours   Serves: 4

DIRECTIONS

In a large bowl, combine the flour, sugar, baking powder, salt, and lemon zest. In another bowl, whisk together the lemon juice, almond milk, melted coconut oil, and vanilla extract. Pour this liquid mixture into the dry ingredients and mix until just combined. Gently fold in the blueberries. Transfer the batter into a greased slow cooker. Cover and cook on high for 3 hours or until a toothpick inserted into the center comes out clean. Allow the cake to cool slightly before serving. It's best served warm, topped with a dollop of vegan whipped cream or ice cream.

NUTRITIONAL INFORMATION

Per serving: 480 calories, 6g protein, 75g carbohydrates, 20g fat, 3g fiber, 0mg cholesterol, 180mg sodium, 150mg potassium.

Maple & Pecan Sticky Buns

INGREDIENTS

- 2 cups all-purpose flour or gluten-free flour
- 2 tsp instant yeast
- 1/4 cup coconut sugar
- 1/2 cup almond milk or other plant-based milk, warmed
- 3 tbsp coconut oil, melted
- 1 tsp vanilla extract
- 1/4 cup maple syrup
- 2 tbsp coconut oil, softened
- 1 cup chopped pecans
- 1 tsp cinnamon
- 1/3 cup maple syrup
- 1/3 cup chopped pecans

 Prep Time: 25 min

 Cook Time: 2 hours

Serves: 6

DIRECTIONS

Combine flour, instant yeast, coconut sugar, warmed almond milk, melted coconut oil, vanilla extract, and a pinch of salt; knead until smooth. Rest for 10 minutes. Roll out dough, spread softened coconut oil, drizzle with 1/4 cup maple syrup, sprinkle pecans and cinnamon. Roll into a log, slice into 6 parts. Pour 1/3 cup maple syrup into greased slow cooker, sprinkle with 1/3 cup pecans. Place sliced buns in slow cooker, cover, cook on high for 2 hours. Flip onto serving platter with pecan and syrup topping on top. Serve warm.

NUTRITIONAL INFORMATION

Per serving: 540 calories, 8g protein, 85g carbohydrates, 22g fat, 4g fiber, 0mg cholesterol, 50mg sodium, 220mg potassium.

Vegan Tiramisu Trifle

INGREDIENTS

- 1 cup all-purpose flour or gluten-free flour
- 1/2 cup coconut sugar
- 1 tsp baking powder
- 1/2 cup almond milk or other plant-based milk
- 1/4 cup coconut oil, melted
- 1 tsp vanilla extract
- 1/2 cup strong brewed coffee, cooled
- 2 tbsp coffee liqueur
- 1 1/2 cups raw cashews, soaked overnight
- 1/2 cup coconut cream
- 1/4 cup maple syrup
- 1 tsp vanilla extract

 Prep Time: 30 min

 Cook Time: 2 hours

 Serves: 4

DIRECTIONS

Combine flour, coconut sugar, and baking powder in a bowl. Gradually add almond milk, melted coconut oil, and vanilla extract; mix to form a smooth batter. Pour into a greased slow cooker. Cook on low for 1.5 hours or until a toothpick comes out clean. Blend soaked cashews, coconut cream, maple syrup, vanilla extract, and a pinch of salt until smooth. Once the cake is done, poke holes with a fork, pour brewed coffee and coffee liqueur over it. Spread cashew cream on top, dust with cocoa powder. Cover and let it sit on 'warm' for 30 minutes to meld flavors.

NUTRITIONAL INFORMATION

Per serving: 650 calories, 10g protein, 75g carbohydrates, 35g fat, 3g fiber, 0mg cholesterol, 80mg sodium, 320mg potassium.

Pear & Cinnamon Compote

INGREDIENTS

- 4 large ripe pears, peeled, cored, and diced
- 1/2 cup coconut sugar or maple syrup
- 1 cup water
- 2 cinnamon sticks
- 1 tsp vanilla extract
- Zest of 1 lemon
- Pinch of salt

Prep Time: 10 min

Cook Time: 3 hours

Serves: 4

DIRECTIONS

In the slow cooker, combine diced pears, coconut sugar or maple syrup, water, cinnamon sticks, vanilla extract, lemon zest, and a pinch of salt. Cover and cook on low for 3 hours, stirring occasionally, until the pears are soft and the liquid has thickened slightly. Remove the cinnamon sticks before serving. The compote can be served warm or chilled. It pairs perfectly with vegan yogurt, oatmeal, or even on its own.

NUTRITIONAL INFORMATION

Per serving: 200 calories, 1g protein, 52g carbohydrates, 0.5g fat, 6g fiber, 0mg cholesterol, 10mg sodium, 215mg potassium.

Beverages & Warmers

Mulled Apple & Cranberry Cider

INGREDIENTS

- 4 cups pure apple cider (unsweetened)
- 1 cup cranberry juice (unsweetened)
- 2 cinnamon sticks
- 1 orange, thinly sliced
- 6 whole cloves
- 1 star anise
- 1/4 cup maple syrup (or adjust to taste)
- A pinch of nutmeg

Prep Time: 10 min

Cook Time: 2 hours

Serves: 4

DIRECTIONS

In the slow cooker, combine apple cider, cranberry juice, cinnamon sticks, orange slices, cloves, star anise, maple syrup, and nutmeg. Cover and cook on low for 2 hours, allowing the flavors to meld together. Before serving, strain the cider to remove the cloves, star anise, and cinnamon sticks. Serve warm in mugs, garnishing with an orange slice if desired.

NUTRITIONAL INFORMATION

Per serving: 150 calories, 0g protein, 38g carbohydrates, 0g fat, 0.5g fiber, 0mg cholesterol, 10mg sodium, 200mg potassium.

Vegan Spiced Hot Chocolate

INGREDIENTS

- 4 cups almond milk (or any other plant-based milk)
- 1/2 cup vegan dark chocolate chips
- 2 tablespoons cocoa powder
- 2 tablespoons maple syrup (or adjust to taste)
- 1 cinnamon stick
- 1/2 teaspoon vanilla extract
- 1/4 teaspoon ground nutmeg
- A pinch of cayenne pepper (optional, for a little kick)

Prep Time: 5 minutes

Cook Time: 2 hours

Serves: 4

DIRECTIONS

In the slow cooker, combine almond milk, dark chocolate chips, cocoa powder, maple syrup, cinnamon stick, vanilla extract, nutmeg, and cayenne pepper. Cover and cook on low for 2 hours, stirring occasionally to ensure the chocolate is well combined. Before serving, remove the cinnamon stick. Serve warm in mugs, garnishing with a sprinkle of cocoa powder or cinnamon on top if desired.

NUTRITIONAL INFORMATION

Per serving: 220 calories, 3g protein, 28g carbohydrates, 11g fat, 3g fiber, 0mg cholesterol, 80mg sodium, 200mg potassium.

Slow-Cooked Golden Turmeric Latte

INGREDIENTS

- 4 cups almond milk (or any other plant-based milk of your choice)
- 1 tablespoon ground turmeric
- 1/2 teaspoon ground cinnamon
- 1/4 teaspoon black pepper (to help with turmeric absorption)
- 1-inch piece of fresh ginger, sliced
- 2 tablespoons maple syrup (or adjust to taste)
- 1 teaspoon vanilla extract
- Coconut whipped cream for topping (optional)

 Prep Time: 5 minutes

 Cook Time: 1 hour 30 minutes

 Serves: 4

DIRECTIONS

In the slow cooker, combine almond milk, turmeric, cinnamon, black pepper, ginger slices, maple syrup, and vanilla extract. Cover and cook on low for 1 hour 30 minutes, stirring occasionally. Before serving, strain out the ginger slices. Serve warm in mugs and top with coconut whipped cream if desired.

NUTRITIONAL INFORMATION

Per serving: 105 calories, 1g protein, 16g carbohydrates, 4g fat, 1g fiber, 0mg cholesterol, 90mg sodium, 150mg potassium.

Warm Lemon & Ginger Elixir

INGREDIENTS

- 5 cups of water
- 1 cup freshly squeezed lemon juice (about 6 lemons)
- 2-inch piece of fresh ginger, thinly sliced
- 2 tablespoons maple syrup (or adjust to taste)
- 1 pinch of cayenne pepper (optional for an extra kick)
- Lemon slices for garnish (optional)

 Prep Time: 10 min

 Cook Time: 2 hours

 Serves: 4

DIRECTIONS

In your slow cooker, combine water, fresh lemon juice, ginger slices, and maple syrup. Cover and set to cook on low for 2 hours. After 2 hours, strain the mixture to remove ginger slices. Serve warm in mugs, garnished with a lemon slice and a pinch of cayenne pepper if desired.

NUTRITIONAL INFORMATION

Per serving: 50 calories, 0.5g protein, 13g carbohydrates, 0.1g fat, 0.2g fiber, 0mg cholesterol, 5mg sodium, 75mg potassium.

Lavender & Chamomile Sleepy Time Tea

INGREDIENTS

- 5 cups of water
- 2 tablespoons dried chamomile flowers
- 2 tablespoons dried lavender buds
- 1 tablespoon maple syrup (optional for a touch of sweetness)
- Fresh lemon slices (optional)

Prep Time: 5 min

Cook Time: 1 hour

Serves: 4

DIRECTIONS

In your slow cooker, combine water, chamomile flowers, and lavender buds. Set the slow cooker to low and allow to simmer for 1 hour. After an hour, strain the tea to remove the chamomile and lavender. Serve warm in mugs with a splash of maple syrup and a lemon slice if desired.

NUTRITIONAL INFORMATION

Per serving: 10 calories, 0g protein, 2.5g carbohydrates, 0g fat, 0g fiber, 0mg cholesterol, 10mg sodium, 12mg potassium.

Spicy Vegan Mexican Hot Chocolate

INGREDIENTS

- 4 cups almond milk (or other plant-based milk of choice)
- 1/2 cup dark chocolate chunks (ensure it's vegan)
- 1/4 cup unsweetened cocoa powder
- 1/4 cup maple syrup or agave nectar
- 1 teaspoon vanilla extract
- 1/4 teaspoon ground cinnamon
- 1/4 teaspoon ground nutmeg
- A pinch of cayenne pepper (adjust to desired heat level)
- A pinch of sea salt

Prep Time: 10 min

Cook Time: 2 hours

Serves: 4

DIRECTIONS

In the slow cooker, combine almond milk, dark chocolate chunks, cocoa powder, maple syrup, and vanilla extract. Whisk until the ingredients are well combined and the chocolate starts melting. Stir in the ground cinnamon, nutmeg, cayenne pepper, and sea salt. Set the slow cooker to low and heat for 2 hours, stirring occasionally. Serve hot with a sprinkle of extra cinnamon on top if desired.

NUTRITIONAL INFORMATION

Per serving: 210 calories, 4g protein, 30g carbohydrates, 12g fat, 4g fiber, 0mg cholesterol, 115mg sodium, 230mg potassium.

Toasted Almond & Vanilla Warmer

INGREDIENTS

- 4 cups almond milk (unsweetened)
- 1/2 cup toasted almonds (chopped)
- 1 vanilla bean (scraped) or 2 teaspoons pure vanilla extract
- 2 tablespoons maple syrup or agave nectar
- A pinch of sea salt
- Cinnamon stick or 1/2 teaspoon ground cinnamon (optional for added warmth)

 Prep Time: 10 minutes

 Cook Time: 1.5 hours

 Serves: 4

DIRECTIONS

In a pan, lightly toast the chopped almonds until they release a nutty aroma. Be careful not to burn them. Add the toasted almonds, almond milk, vanilla bean contents (or vanilla extract), and maple syrup to the slow cooker. Stir well to combine. Set the slow cooker to low and let the mixture warm for 1.5 hours. If using a cinnamon stick, add it during this step. Before serving, remove the vanilla bean pod (if used) and the cinnamon stick, then pour into mugs and enjoy.

NUTRITIONAL INFORMATION

Per serving: 150 calories, 5g protein, 15g carbohydrates, 9g fat, 2g fiber, 0mg cholesterol, 180mg sodium, 240mg potassium.

Slow-Cooked Chai Latte

INGREDIENTS

- 4 cups almond milk (unsweetened)
- 2 black tea bags or 2 tablespoons loose leaf black tea
- 4 green cardamom pods (cracked)
- 2 cinnamon sticks
- 4 whole cloves
- 2 slices fresh ginger
- 1 star anise
- 1/4 teaspoon whole black peppercorns
- 2 tablespoons maple syrup or agave nectar
- 1 teaspoon pure vanilla extract

 Prep Time: 10 min

 Cook Time: 2 hours

 Serves: 4

DIRECTIONS

Add almond milk, black tea, cardamom pods, cinnamon sticks, cloves, ginger, star anise, black peppercorns, and maple syrup to the slow cooker. Set the slow cooker to low and let the mixture steep for 2 hours. 30 minutes before serving, stir in the vanilla extract. Before serving, strain the mixture to remove the spices and tea, then pour into mugs and enjoy. Optionally, you can froth a little extra almond milk and top each cup for added creaminess.

NUTRITIONAL INFORMATION

Per serving: 90 calories, 2g protein, 15g carbohydrates, 3g fat, 1g fiber, 0mg cholesterol, 150mg sodium, 200mg potassium.

Pomegranate & Rosemary Winter Punch

INGREDIENTS

- 4 cups pomegranate juice (unsweetened)
- 1 cup sparkling water (to be added before serving)
- 2 sprigs fresh rosemary
- 1 orange, sliced
- 1/4 cup maple syrup (adjust to taste)
- 2 tablespoons lemon juice
- 1 cinnamon stick
- 1/2 cup fresh pomegranate arils

 Prep Time: 15 minutes

 Cook Time: 2 hours

 Serves: 4

DIRECTIONS

In the slow cooker, combine the pomegranate juice, rosemary sprigs, orange slices, maple syrup, lemon juice, and cinnamon stick. Set the slow cooker to low and allow the flavors to meld for 2 hours. Prior to serving, strain the punch to remove the solid ingredients and pour it back into the slow cooker to keep warm. Add the sparkling water and pomegranate arils to the punch, stirring gently to combine. Serve in mugs or glasses, garnishing with additional rosemary or orange slices if desired.

NUTRITIONAL INFORMATION

Per serving: 120 calories, 1g protein, 30g carbohydrates, 0.5g fat, 0.5g fiber, 0mg cholesterol, 30mg sodium, 500mg potassium.

Vegan Creamy Matcha Latte

INGREDIENTS

- 4 cups unsweetened almond milk (or any plant-based milk of choice)
- 2 teaspoons high-quality matcha powder
- 1/4 cup hot water
- 1/4 cup maple syrup (or adjust to taste)
- 1 teaspoon vanilla extract
- A pinch of sea salt

  Prep Time: 10 min

 Cook Time: 30 minutes

 Serves: 4

DIRECTIONS

In a small bowl, whisk together the matcha powder and hot water until it forms a smooth paste without any lumps. In the slow cooker, add almond milk, the matcha paste, maple syrup, vanilla extract, and a pinch of sea salt. Stir to combine. Cover and cook on the low setting for 30 minutes, ensuring it doesn't boil. Before serving, whisk the latte well to ensure it's frothy and fully combined. Serve in mugs and, if desired, sprinkle a little matcha on top for garnish.

NUTRITIONAL INFORMATION

Per serving: 95 calories, 1g protein, 18g carbohydrates, 2.5g fat, 1g fiber, 0mg cholesterol, 180mg sodium, 300mg potassium.

Herbal Immunity Broth

INGREDIENTS

- 8 cups water
- 1 large onion, roughly chopped
- 3 cloves garlic, minced
- 2 inches fresh ginger, sliced
- 1 inch fresh turmeric, sliced (or 1 tsp ground turmeric)
- 2 tablespoons dried shiitake mushrooms
- 1 small bunch of fresh parsley
- 1 tablespoon dried echinacea
- 1 tablespoon dried astragalus root

Prep Time: 15 minutes

Cook Time: 4 hours

Serves: 4

DIRECTIONS

In your slow cooker, add all ingredients except salt and pepper. Cover with the 8 cups of water. Set the slow cooker on low and let the broth simmer for 4 hours. Once done, strain out the solids and season the broth with salt and pepper if desired. Serve hot and enjoy as a comforting immunity-boosting drink.

NUTRITIONAL INFORMATION

Per serving: 35 calories, 1g protein, 8g carbohydrates, 0.2g fat, 1.5g fiber, 0mg cholesterol, 20mg sodium, 250mg potassium.

Spiced Berry & Red Wine Brew

INGREDIENTS

- 1 bottle (750 ml) vegan red wine (such as Cabernet Sauvignon or Merlot)
- 2 cups mixed fresh or frozen berries (raspberries, blackberries, blueberries)
- 1 orange, sliced
- 3 cinnamon sticks
- 4 whole cloves
- 2 star anise
- 1/4 cup agave nectar or maple syrup (adjust to taste)
- 1/2 cup water
- A pinch of nutmeg

Prep Time: 10 min

Cook Time: 3 hours

Serves: 4

DIRECTIONS

In the slow cooker, combine red wine, mixed berries, orange slices, cinnamon sticks, cloves, star anise, agave or maple syrup, and water. Set the cooker on low and let it simmer for 3 hours. About 15 minutes before serving, sprinkle in the nutmeg and stir gently. Strain out the solids and serve the brew warm in mugs or glasses.

NUTRITIONAL INFORMATION

Per serving: 240 calories, 0.5g protein, 35g carbohydrates, 0.1g fat, 2.5g fiber, 0mg cholesterol, 10mg sodium, 200mg potassium.

Caramel & Cinnamon Coffee Delight

INGREDIENTS

- 4 cups freshly brewed coffee
- 1 cup almond milk (or any other plant-based milk)
- 1/4 cup vegan caramel sauce (available at health food stores or online)
- 1 teaspoon ground cinnamon
- 1/4 teaspoon vanilla extract
- Whipped coconut cream for topping (optional)
- Cinnamon sticks for garnish (optional)
- A pinch of sea salt

 Prep Time: 10 minutes

 Cook Time: 2 hours

 Serves: 4

DIRECTIONS

In the slow cooker, combine the brewed coffee, almond milk, vegan caramel sauce, ground cinnamon, and vanilla extract. Set the cooker to low and allow the mixture to heat for 2 hours, stirring occasionally. Just before serving, stir in a pinch of sea salt to enhance the caramel flavor. Serve in mugs topped with whipped coconut cream and garnished with a cinnamon stick, if desired.

NUTRITIONAL INFORMATION

Per serving: 90 calories, 1g protein, 18g carbohydrates, 1.5g fat, 1g fiber, 0mg cholesterol, 80mg sodium, 150mg potassium.

Vegan Pumpkin Spice Latte

INGREDIENTS

- 4 cups brewed coffee
- 2 cups almond milk (or any other plant-based milk of choice)
- 1/2 cup pumpkin puree (ensure it's pure pumpkin without additives)
- 1/4 cup maple syrup (or adjust to taste)
- 1 teaspoon pumpkin pie spice
- 1 teaspoon vanilla extract
- Whipped coconut cream for topping (optional)
- A pinch of sea salt
- Cinnamon sticks or ground cinnamon for garnish

 Prep Time: 10 minutes

 Cook Time: 2 hours

 Serves: 4

DIRECTIONS

In your slow cooker, whisk together the brewed coffee, almond milk, pumpkin puree, maple syrup, pumpkin pie spice, and vanilla extract until well combined. Set the cooker to low and let the mixture heat for 2 hours, stirring occasionally. Before serving, add a pinch of sea salt to enhance the flavors. Pour into mugs, top with whipped coconut cream, and sprinkle with cinnamon or garnish with a cinnamon stick if desired.

NUTRITIONAL INFORMATION

Per serving: 120 calories, 2g protein, 25g carbohydrates, 2g fat, 2g fiber, 0mg cholesterol, 90mg sodium, 200mg potassium.

Dark Chocolate & Peppermint Warmer

INGREDIENTS

- 4 cups unsweetened almond milk (or any other plant-based milk of choice)
- 200g dark chocolate (vegan, at least 70% cocoa)
- 1/4 cup maple syrup (or adjust to taste)
- 1/2 teaspoon peppermint extract
- Pinch of sea salt
- Vegan whipped cream for topping (optional)
- Crushed vegan peppermint candies or fresh mint leaves for garnish (optional)

Prep Time: 10 minutes

Cook Time: 3 hours

Serves: 4

DIRECTIONS

In the slow cooker, add almond milk, dark chocolate, and maple syrup. Stir to combine. Cover and set the slow cooker to low heat. Let the mixture heat for about 3 hours, stirring occasionally to ensure the chocolate melts smoothly into the milk. A few minutes before serving, stir in the peppermint extract and sea salt. Serve in mugs, topped with vegan whipped cream, and sprinkle with crushed peppermint candies or garnish with fresh mint leaves if desired.

NUTRITIONAL INFORMATION

Per serving: 250 calories, 4g protein, 32g carbohydrates, 13g fat, 3g fiber, 0mg cholesterol, 80mg sodium, 310mg potassium.

Measurement Conversion Charts

MEASUREMENT

Cup	Ounces	Milliliters	Tablespoons
8 cups	64 oz	1895 ml	128
6 cups	48 oz	1420 ml	96
5 cups	40 oz	1180 ml	80
4 cups	32 oz	960 ml	64
2 cups	16 oz	480 ml	32
1 cup	8 oz	240 ml	16
3/4 cup	6 oz	177 ml	12
2/3 cup	5 oz	158 ml	11
1/2 cup	4 oz	118 ml	8
3/8 cup	3 oz	90 ml	6
1/3 cup	2.5 oz	79 ml	5.5
1/4 cup	2 oz	59 ml	4
1/8 cup	1 oz	30 ml	3
1/16 cup	1/2 oz	15 ml	1

WEIGHT

Imperial	Metric
1/2 oz	15 g
1 oz	29 g
2 oz	57 g
3 oz	85 g
4 oz	113 g
5 oz	141 g
6 oz	170 g
8 oz	227 g
10 oz	283 g
12 oz	340 g
13 oz	369 g
14 oz	397 g
15 oz	425 g
1 lb	453 g

TEMPERATURE

Fahrenheit	Celsius
100 °F	37 °C
150 °F	65 °C
200 °F	93 °C
250 °F	121 °C
300 °F	150 °C
325 °F	160 °C
350 °F	180 °C
375 °F	190 °C
400 °F	200 °C
425 °F	220 °C
450 °F	230 °C
500 °F	260 °C
525 °F	274 °C
550 °F	288 °C

Made in the USA
Las Vegas, NV
07 October 2024

96436619R00063